THE POWER IN OUR HANDS

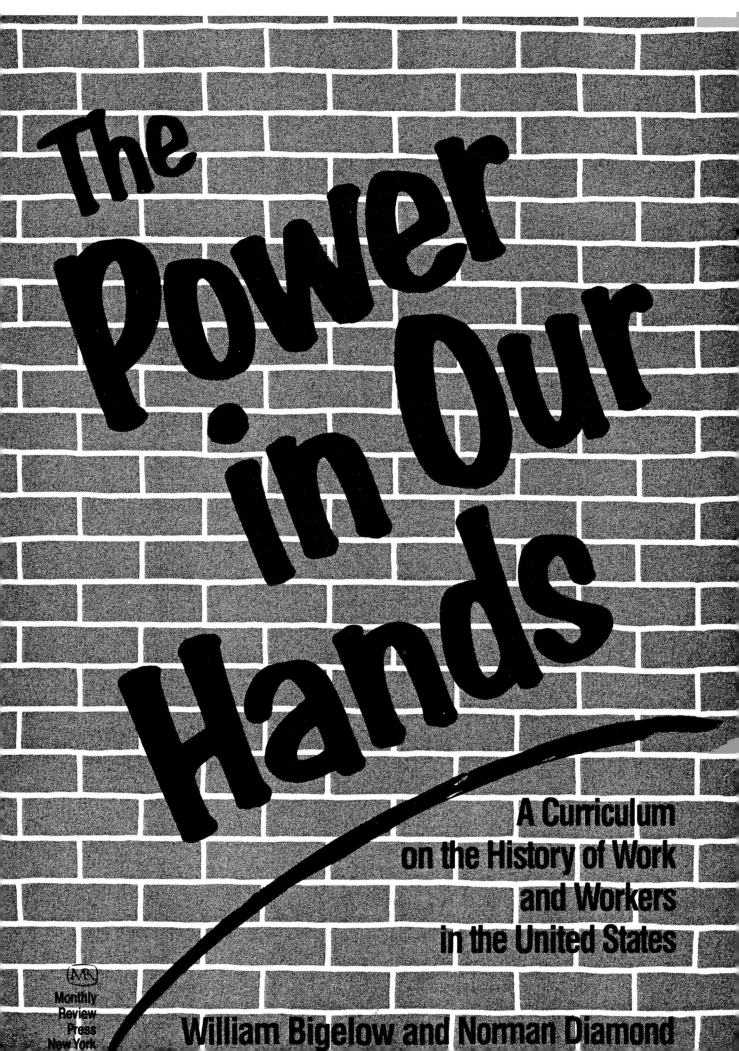

The Power in Our Hands

A Curriculum on the History of Work and Workers in the United States

William Bigelow and Norman Diamond

Monthly Review Press
New York

The art not otherwise credited in the text comes from the following sources:
page 92, from Fred Wright, *So Long, Partner!* (New York: United Electrical,
Radio, and Machine Workers of America, 1975); pages 104 and 116, from
Richard B. Morris, ed., *The U.S. Department of Labor History of the
American Worker* (Washington, D.C.: U.S. Government Printing Office,
1976); page 111, drawing by Thomas Hart Benton from Leo Huberman, *We,
the People* (New York: Monthly Review Press, 1960); page 119, from John
Grafton, *New York in the Nineteenth Century* (New York: Dover Publications,
1977); pages 125, 132, and 134, from William Cahn, *Lawrence 1912: The
Bread and Roses Strike* (New York: Pilgrim Press, 1980); pages 140 and 144,
from *Roll the Union On: A Pictorial History of the Southern Tenant Farmers' Union*
(Chicago: Charles H. Kerr, 1987); page 147, from William Cahn, *A Pictorial History
of American Labor* (New York: Crown Publishers, 1972); page 150, from Roger
Buchanan, *Dock Strike: History of the 1934 Waterfront Strike in Portland, Oregon*
(Everett, WA: The Working Press, 1975); pages 159 and 160, drawings by
Bits Hayden from Mike Quin, *The Big Strike* (New York: International
Publishers, 1979).

Library of Congress Cataloging-in-Publication Data

The power in our hands.

1. Labor and laboring classes—United States—
History—Study and teaching (Secondary).   2. Labor
and laboring classes—United States—History—Study
and teaching (Higher).
I. Bigelow, William
II. Title.
HD8066.B48   1988   331'.0973   88-13365
ISBN 0-85345-753-0
ISBN 0-85345-754-9 (student handbook)

Monthly Review Press
122 West 27th Street, New York, N.Y. 10001

Manufactured in the United States of America

10 9 8 7 6 5 4 3 2 1

In our hands is placed a power greater than their hoarded gold . . .
We can bring to birth a new world from the ashes of the old.

—Ralph Chaplin
Solidarity Forever (1915)

To the memory of Warren Plaut (1951–1987),
President of Graphic Communications International Union Local 48B,
whose life exemplified what this book is about.

CONTENTS

Student Handouts

ACKNOWLEDGMENTS

There are a number of sayings we're all familiar with that heap contempt on group effort: too many cooks spoil the broth; a camel is a horse designed by committee; too many chiefs, not enough Indians. Yet when it comes to writing and testing curriculum, the more cooks, committees, and chiefs, the better.

The lessons in this guide have been touched by many hands. In 1978, Jerry Lembcke and Leigh Bradford-Ratterree, then on the staff of the Pacific Northwest Labor College, assembled high school teachers and labor educators from the region to share lesson plans and methodologies on teaching labor history. These monthly meetings culminated in a week-long seminar which brought together labor organizers, high school and college teachers, historians, and community activists. To enable this gathering, The Oregon Committee for the Humanities provided generous financial assistance. A number of the participants in those early sessions influenced the direction of this effort and have continued to offer valuable advice. We especially want to thank Tom McKenna and Peter Thacker. In addition, one of the first lessons we produced, the *1934 West Coast Longshore Strike*, was co-written by Sally Tollefson.

From the beginning, Millie Thayer wrote and tested the curriculum, and led workshops with other teachers. Her experience and creativity have directly or indirectly contributed to every lesson included here.

At a time when the curriculum was first taking shape, Jerry Baum and Marty Hart-Landsberg met with us regularly. Their counsel, grounded in labor education experience and dedication to labor culture, enriched our conception of this book.

An earlier draft of this guide was distributed by the Pacific Northwest Labor College. In 1982, PNLC sponsored a day-long workshop for twenty-five area teachers who agreed to test the lessons in their classrooms. Once again, The Oregon Committee for the Humanities came to our financial assistance to enable this further testing.

A number of the writing assignments included in the curriculum were inspired by Linda Christensen, a teacher at Jefferson High School in Portland and the most imaginative writing instructor we know.

As labor organizer and teacher, Jeff Edmundson gave us useful advice from his experiences with the lessons. He also kindly allowed us to use his "Confessions of a French-Fry Champion" (**Lesson #7: Taylorizing Burgers: A Fantasy**).

Fellow members of the Portland Labor Players II, a group that combined quality theater with a commitment to its audience of working people, provided moral support and more. In particular, Robin Chilstrom, Jane Ferguson, Marita Keys, Kath Meardon, Melinda Pittman, Marie Selland, and Vicki Stolsen enhanced our sense that playfulness, too, is essential in learning.

As we readied the manuscript for publication we received valuable editorial assistance from Martha Gaston Bigelow, Elizabeth Robinson, Dave Forrest, Bill Resnick, and Sy Adler. The American Friends Service Committee in Portland graciously allowed us to use its office for editing.

Timely encouragement and advice came from Kassahun Checole of Africa World Press; Keith Johnson of the International Woodworkers of America; Jim Thompson of the Association of Western Pulp and Paper Workers; Dick Edgington of the International Chemical Workers; Roger Auerbach of the American Federation of State, County, and Municipal Employees; Roger Honig of the International Association of Ironworkers; Lou Stewart of the Washington State Labor Council; Gene Klare, editor of the *Oregon* (now *Northwest*) *Labor Press;* Jan Haaken of the Work Psychology program at Portland State University; Bob Boyer and Judy Knawls of the A. Philip Randolph Institute; and Julia Ruutilla, longtime labor activist and writer for *The Dispatcher,* newspaper of the International Longshoremen and Warehousemen's Union.

Thanks also to Susan Lowes, Jon Steinberg, and Monthly Review Press for their vision in risking an unfamiliar project . . . simply because they think it worthwhile.

And more than thanks to Patricia Kullberg for her warm blend of emotional and political support and for the stimulation provided by her own projects; and to Alexander Kullberg Diamond, eighteen months, insistent on breaking his papa's absorption in writing and reminding him of the joys and potential of what our effort is for.

Publication of this curriculum does not stop the process of refinement and addition. For this, we count on you, the teacher, community organizer, labor educator. Throughout the years that we have been engaged in labor education, our inspiration to continue work on this curriculum has come from our colleagues—you. As you teach the lessons in this book, please take some time to complete the evaluation. Help us develop a community of educators committed to creating a pedagogy for democracy.

NOTES TO THE TEACHER

The lessons in this book are the product of more than ten years of testing and revision. They've been used in middle and high schools, colleges, workshops with teachers and community activists, union apprenticeship classes, labor education courses, meetings of union organizations, and worker study groups. We hope and expect that educators at all these levels will find this book of use.

For each of these levels the book might have been organized slightly differently. We've chosen to present it as a high school curriculum, the format most easily adaptable to other uses. Thus we say "student" and "teacher" throughout, whereas "participant" and "facilitator" or "workshop coordinator" might be more appropriate to nonschool contexts. Similarly, the "lessons" are divided into periods ("Day One," "Day Two," etc.) of less than an hour, but they can easily be combined in one session. In any case, the time indicated for each lesson is only an approximation. Because the lessons encourage extensive student participation, our own experience has shown that the timing will vary from one use to the next.

Each lesson includes detailed instructions, student materials, questions for discussion, and suggested follow-up activities. The book is divided in two parts. The first includes teacher instructions, the second the student handouts. The second part is also available separately, as a Student Handbook.

How to Read a Curriculum

A curriculum doesn't read from start to finish like a novel. Because each lesson describes a group learning experience, you'll most likely find the book easiest to follow if you encounter the activities as a group would. In a role play, for example, when the instructions call for students to receive roles, take a break from reading the instructions to look over some of the roles. We've found this helps to imagine the activity.

If you're like us, the introduction to a book sometimes gets read, sometimes not. In the introduction to this curriculum we share some of our experiences with the lessons and outline obstacles and possibilities in teaching labor history. It is what we wish we knew before launching this project. We've also included a brief introduction to each lesson which offers an overview of its goals and objectives.

"What If I Don't Have Time to Teach It All?"

For a class that meets 45–50 minutes a day, five days a week, the sixteen lessons would require about seven weeks. That's a long time. Nonetheless, we hope that you will consider using the book in its entirety for a number of reasons. First, each lesson builds upon and reinforces earlier lessons; there is an integrity to the scope and sequencing of the full sixteen. Second, while ours is a study of the history of work and workers, in fact it's much more. As we stress and elaborate in the introduction, the lessons are really explorations into the meaning and mechanics of democracy. Further, the curriculum helps participants gain a sharper analysis of the entire society. All this means that there is a lot more going on than simply labor history.

Okay—there's the plea. Still, some of you will not have sufficient time to cover the entire curriculum. The following is our abbreviated, no-frills version:

Lesson #1: Organic Goodie Simulation

Lesson #2: Who Makes History?

Lesson #4: Paper Airplane Simulation

Lesson #10: Lawrence, 1912: The Singing Strike

Lesson #12: Southern Tenant Farmers' Union: Black and White Unite?

Lesson #14: Union Maids

INTRODUCTION

THE POWER IN OUR HANDS:
CONTENT, PEDAGOGY, AND STUDENT EXPERIENCE

*What would it mean to live
in a city whose people were changing
each other's despair into hope?—
You yourself must change it.—
What would it feel like to know
your country was changing?—
You yourself must change it.—
Though your life felt arduous
new and unmapped and strange
what would it mean to stand on the first
page of the end of despair?*

—Adrienne Rich

To teach is to be a warrior against cynicism and despair. We lose battles daily: A student comments that all people are selfish and out for themselves; a fellow staff member confides, "That woman is beyond hope." Last year, one of our students attempted suicide with Drano and orange juice.

We've joined the fight in different decades and at different points. One of us is a high school teacher, the other a college professor and labor educator. We share the goal of having our teaching contribute to the creation of a fully democratic society in which people have power and hope. To this end, we see an understanding of labor's heritage and of the strengths of working-class culture as crucial. Crucial also are skills of informed and effective participation: to be able to analyze and take action.

When we first began teaching, we were not as well aware that *how* we teach, as well as *what* we teach, is part of our work against cynicism and implies a larger social vision. We learned quickly that a "we talk, you listen/read this and answer the questions" pedagogy anticipates an undemocratic outcome. Top-down education, like the hierarchical power pyramids people experience in work and community, erodes self-esteem and initiative and promotes feelings of apathy. Apathetic people don't change society—or themselves.

Too often, our early attempts to find alternatives proved disappointing. When one of us was a first-year teacher, his well-intentioned, if awkward, efforts prompted a student to remark, "This class is weird; it feels like a local TV ad." We made an obvious discovery: critical and participatory teaching is a lot tougher to pull off than conventional classroom methods. At times, sheer exhaustion drove us to the havens of traditional passivity-producing lessons.

We began experimenting with the lessons that ultimately became this curriculum, sobered by disappointments yet still committed to democratic education. Now, years later and after much trial and testing, we think we're making progress.

The Power in Our Hands: As the title suggests, the curriculum encourages participants—students,* workers, teachers—to reflect on our power, our ability to make and remake society—indeed to see *everything* about our lives as changeable. In its treatment of history, the curriculum focuses on the contributions of ordinary people—the "hired hands"—as builders and creators. It's really a curriculum on

---

*For the sake of convenience, we use the term "students" throughout the introduction to mean all participants in the activities other than the teacher or group leader. When we use the term more narrowly to mean high school or college students, this should be clear from the context.

democracy, an extended exploration in participation and decision-making.

The lessons in the curriculum do not, however, impose a perspective on students—even one that argues for democracy. Rather, students confront the difficult choices that genuine democracy requires. They engage in dialogue with the content, each other, and the teacher to make personal the ideas in the lessons. It is a students-centered curriculum: they think, they choose, they act.

In the three upcoming sections of this introduction we summarize how (1) *the content*, (2) *the teaching methodology*, and (3) *the use of student experience* contribute to creating a classroom of active learning and student empowerment:

• The content of the curriculum highlights instances where people acted together to understand and change the conditions of their lives. Drawing on history, students learn some of the skills of social analysis that make informed action possible. They learn to examine and challenge their own and others' premises about people's capabilities; they learn how change occurs and what social change is possible.

• The learning methodology in the lessons is participatory. Through role play, simulation, and imaginative writing, students move into the hearts and minds of the characters who worked for and against change. They encounter history not as an inevitability but as a range of possible outcomes dependent largely on the understandings and efforts of people like themselves.

• And the students' own lives become an additional "text" within the lessons. In writing and discussion, students are asked to examine their experiences as a way to root the concepts of the curriculum in their own lives. The lessons draw on students' experiences to understand history, and draw on history to understand the students' experiences.

The Content: Change Is Possible

Most people spend more time in work than any other single activity. Work is crucial in shaping people's attitudes and sense of their own capabilities. And the structure of work strongly influences other social institutions, including school and family. Students are forever hearing parents and teachers admonish, "This will prepare you for getting a job," or "Your boss wouldn't let you get away with that."

Too often, that work world is presented as an unquestioned fact of life—or even as life itself. The lessons here call on the participants to take a critical look, to ask whether alternative structures could exist. And to the extent that social institutions mirror the organization of work, students gain insights into other important influences on their lives.

Not a "Great Men" History of Labor. Many textbooks and union histories focus on "great men." Cigar-chomping Sam Gompers and blustery George Meany conferring with presidents can be colorful characters, but when we lionize famous individuals, we tend to forget underlying social forces and the decisions and actions taken by ordinary workers—people like our students and their families. Overemphasizing the contributions of great men can discourage students from identifying with people like themselves who reflected on their lives and decided to act.

Recently, for example, we visited the classes of a friend in Los Angeles. In her school's U.S. history textbook, the obligatory chapter on the rise of the 1930s union movement gave credit almost exclusively to leaders like John L. Lewis and Phillip Murray. The book's real hero was President Roosevelt, without whom, the authors apparently believe, little change would have occurred. Never mind that Roosevelt's vision of change was sharply at odds with that of many workers—the text ignored those workers almost entirely. In this book and in too much other labor history—indeed, in too much history in general—change is bestowed from above rather than struggled for and, at least in part, enacted from below.

In this curriculum, when we feature the achievements of individuals (the remarkable story of former Klansman C.P. Ellis, for example—see **Lesson #12: Southern Tenant Farmers' Union: Black and White Unite?**) it is to demonstrate the capacity of ordinary people to learn and change. We highlight individuals not for their fame but for what their stories can teach students about their own capabilities.

We've also chosen historical episodes that challenge widely held beliefs about the inability of people from diverse backgrounds to work together for change. Workers speaking dozens of languages, many illiterate, a large proportion teenagers, *did* unite in the 1912 Lawrence, Massachusetts, textile strike. Our students are usually surprised; they aren't accustomed to organizing for even such modest goals as better cafeteria food or their own workplace bulletin board. Tracking, grading, class backgrounds, and sometimes tastes in music, as well as age, race, and sex differences, discourage high school and college students and workers from attempting to act together. We see them interpret history through these same cracked lenses. Although rarely more than a footnote in most history texts, the Lawrence strike can spark deep reconsideration of people's potential to work through the divisions among them.

Racial Conflict. Racial antagonisms also often seem to students to be part of human nature. In **It's a Mystery (Lesson #11),** we explore some of the causes of this and see which social groups actually gain from racial hostilities. Again, our goal is to encourage students to understand racism as they understand other divisions: as phenomena with comprehensible social origins. In the **Southern Tenants Farmers' Union,** students write a dialogue from the point of view of farmers who need racial unity to accomplish their goal but also need to overcome long-held antagonisms. Here, as throughout the curriculum, students

see no certainty of positive change, only a possibility dependent on people's efforts and choices.

In one dialogue, a student named Jeff had two black farmers square off. Here is an excerpt:

Tom: Frank, you ain't making no sense. Why should I join this union?

Frank: Tom, if you do, then other black brothers will join. Soon all the blacks would be in the union. Then and only then would we be able to control the planters instead of them controlling us.

Tom: Frank, this gun is all the control I need. I can do anything I want if I got this gun.

Frank: Can you keep your job with that gun? Can that gun help you out when you're starving? Can that gun keep your family together? Can you feed yourself with that gun? No. The gun you have there just keeps you from trusting folks enough to give them half a chance to help you.

Tom: Frank, I just see a bunch of white men wanting my five dollars. There ain't no white man going to go out of his way for a black man. Wasn't ever like that, never will be like that.

Tom eventually joins the union, but without enthusiasm. Jeff acted out his dialogue with another student and helped lead a discussion about why Tom maintained his attitudes and whether Frank could have used more persuasive arguments. The discussion allowed us to explore student beliefs about the possibility of black-white unity. But discussions like this require some trust among students, and beginning with the history helps give perspective and critical distance from our own lives.

The Causes of Social Injustice. Students are tempted to blame oppressive conditions on the selfish inclinations of this or that individual. For example, the "greedy" owner in the **Organic Goodie Simulation (Lesson #1)** and Andrew Carnegie in **Homestead (Lesson #8)** are easy targets. Too easy. We've included questions in the lessons that encourage students to move beyond simplistic explanations to consider the structural reasons for injustice. In the **1934 West Coast Longshore Strike**

(**Lesson #13**), for example, the waterfront employers cut wages to $.85 an hour and require thirty-six-hour shifts. But the cause is systemic: owners face sharp competition for the scarce 1930s shipping business. "Nice" owners will go under. The system is the problem, not evil people.

Too often, on the rare occasions that labor history is taught, the point seems to be to show students how awful things were "back then" and how lucky we are now. For example, the film **Union Maids (Lesson #14)** could be misused to show only the terrible hardships of the 1930s, that tough struggles were necessary, great victories won, and thank heaven it's all in the past. Our approach reflects the filmmakers' own attempt to look at the 1930s from the standpoint of activists still alive today, still feisty and committed to social change. Students not only see a decade of determined and courageous labor activity, but they also examine the 1930s goals not yet accomplished and think about lessons for today.

Visions of Work and Workers. Before joining the workforce, students' study of work is generally confined to "career education." At the high school where one of us teaches, career education is a required subject. The text for the course encourages adjustment, not critical thinking. As one teacher told us, "The book says, 'Here's the way it is; fit in as best you can. Dress right, don't talk back.' "

The mass media are worse. In one study, the International Association of Machinists monitored television programming—members across the country noted all TV references to work and workers. The results: work itself is nearly always ignored; "workers" are usually presented simplistically and as stereotypes—as beer-drinking caricatures who butcher the English language and vegetate in front of the TV.

These omissions and stereotypes lead students and young workers to hold their own backgrounds in contempt. If we fail to challenge the negative social messages, we contribute to reinforcing these attitudes. Work must be

seen as an area for analysis and reflection. If not, people will be disabled in assessing or influencing a major part of their lives.

A workshop we offered recently included people from an assortment of unions and occupations. A sheetmetal worker complained about the negotiating team for his union: "They're just a bunch of guys like me. They should bring in college-educated people. Workers aren't smart enough. The owners always out-talk us so we never get what we want." This expression of self-contempt is a mighty vote of no-confidence in democracy, bred and reinforced in school and media. Unless made explicit and put in context it becomes self-fulfilling: workers who *believe* they cannot control their own affairs in fact cannot.

Challenging Self-Contempt. *The Power in Our Hands* focuses on how changes in work have eroded worker self-confidence. For example, in **Free to Think, Talk, Listen, or Sing (Lesson #5)** students learn that between the Civil War and the early 1900s work was increasingly subdivided, with many jobs becoming more repetitive and machine-like. Students reflect on how these new conditions limited workers' skill development, social interactions, and ultimately their ability to act together for common goals.

Most texts portray changes in work, tools, and machinery as products of "scientific advance" or "brilliant ideas." This curriculum shows how new production techniques were shaped by people with particular motives and interests, often responding to workers' movements and to resistance within the workplace. For example, in **Free to Think, Talk, Listen, or Sing** when mule-spinners began to "trouble" the management of one nineteenth-century mill, the owners brought in new machinery in order to replace male workers with young women—who they expected would prove more docile. As students encounter this history, the "we're not smart enough" attitudes gain some needed context. They can understand these notions as a partial—but intended—consequence of the degraded conditions of work.

The Best Teacher: Experience

A history of people's attempts to work together creatively to better their lives needs a pedagogy to match. In the lessons included here students encounter historical issues first-hand, through simulation, role play, and imaginative writing. Instead of *hearing about,* they *experience.*

In the **Organic Goodie Simulation,** students-as-workers confront an owner (played by the teacher) intent on pitting workers against one another so as to drive down wages. What should we do, students wonder, shut up and do as we're told, beg higher wages from the owner, start a union? Students choose their own strategy. In some classes, the students have sat and watched as the unemployed starve. In others, they have organized an alliance of workers and unemployed to strike. Occasionally, students have taken over the machine and decided to run it themselves. One year students carted us off to a makeshift prison and threatened "death" if we tried to overthrow their new owner-less society.

In the writing assignment following the simulation, participants evaluate their responses to the owner's strategies. With hindsight, students often wonder whether they might have devised a more creative form of resistance. The previous day's struggles, compromises, starvation, and revolts become a rich text for analysis in follow-up discussion.

Simulating Changes in Work. In most labor histories, struggles are portrayed with little reference to the actual work or methods of production. Historically, the organization of work has been both prod and obstacle to workers' efforts for greater democracy. In the **Paper Airplane Simulation (Lesson #4),** highly skilled paper airplane workers watch as the management "steals" their techniques of production, chops up the work process, and reassigns discrete tasks to each worker.

What motivated these changes? Could worker resistance have blocked or redirected them? How would the new organization of the workplace alter workers' family lives or their relationships with one another? Instead of hearing a lecture or reading a handout, students use their own experiences as the basis for probing these and other questions. From having produced paper airplanes, they know that nothing in the nature of the product necessitated that each worker be allowed to make only one fold again and again. They can see what dictated this work organization: the interests and power of management. They understand that the structure of a workplace and the kind of skills workers are allowed to learn and perform are less matters of science or technology than of human choice.

Students *and* Workers. Don, Gary, and Tony are members of the Ironworkers' union. After their apprenticeship class one night, they invited us out for coffee. Their group had just finished **Unit II: Changes in the Workplace/ "Scientific" Management,** and they had some concerns. The conversation lasted hours as they talked about changes in the shop where they worked. "The older workers," one of them said, "each do one kind of job. They're either a welder or a fitter or a burner or a something else. They know how to do other jobs, but they're not certified so they can't actually do them. Now, we're training to do every part of a job, like to build a complete section of a bridge the way a Shopman used to."

At first, as we had studied the history, they had been puzzled. Was their workplace returning to a nineteenth-century mode of production, where workers were masters of the entire process? After **"Taylorizing" Burgers: A Fantasy (Lesson #7),** they concluded that they were going to be used as "serial specialists," never doing more than a fragment of a job. Management, however, would gain increased flexibility with a smaller workforce, because the new workers could be easily moved from one task to another. Their analysis led to an important discussion over staffing and work rules in the next round of contract negotiations.

Among our high school students the most common work is in fast-food restaurants. Richard, who had won an award for "fastest burger flipper," wrote in his year-end evaluation that the highlight of the class was sharing his analysis of why the company offered these kinds of awards. He compared it to the contest that management set up in the **Paper Airplane Simulation.** Likewise, Peggy, who had worked for two years in a pizza parlor, wrote of how amazed she was to think of her day-to-day worklife as part of a larger historical process. She hated work, but thought of job conditions as "just the way things are." Now she was talking with co-workers about their dissatisfactions and what could be changed.

And that's an important goal of the curriculum: the more our students view the world of work—indeed every social institution—as largely the outcome of human decision, the closer they come to realizing the possibility of restructuring these institutions in their interests.

Doing Democracy. In **Lawrence, 1912: The Singing Strike (Lesson #10),** students confront the actual dilemmas faced by the striking millworkers, members of the Industrial Workers of the World (IWW). And like the millworkers, the student strikers must figure out how to feed starving children and confront bayonet-happy militiamen, with no higher authority guiding their deliberations. They must also devise methods to make decisions democratically. These discussions can get heated. We've had students vote to remove unruly peers, divide into competing factions, and turn on haughty, self-appointed leaders.

Students also carry conflicts, petty and deep, into their proceedings. As Brenda wrote in her role play evaluation: "The class brought in outside problems and prejudices. This created a lot of friction. People were learning a new skill and felt they were falling flat on their faces. They were discouraged, but the class was really progressing." Another student wrote, "As soon as someone said, 'Hey man, I think we have too many personal grudges and too much racism in this classroom in order to make decisions together,' I knew we were in for a lot of trouble."

Far from being a distraction, this classroom conflict helps students understand the difficulties Italians, Hungarians, Poles, and a dozen other nationalities had making decisions as a group. After the first set of problems, students step out of their roles to talk about class dynamics and to review the social vision of the IWW which powered the strike. In round two, after this important intervening discussion, students begin to learn what encourages group decision-making and what inhibits it. And by the time students encounter the employers' "God and Country" campaign at the conclusion of the strike, their group problem-solving is downright proficient. As Brenda concluded in her evaluation, "I felt that the class was very successful after the first set of questions. We finally had a chance to find out how to operate without an authority figure. Just like a colt trying out its shaky new legs. After a few spills it can walk around a little."

Students often catch the irreverent egalitarianism of the IWW members they portray. One year a class making decisions was taking longer than we wanted. We (foolishly) put a time limit on the discussion. One youngster shot back, "We don't have to obey that rule—we didn't make it. We're the IWW, we believe in democracy!"

Thinking and talking effectively with one another, weighing evidence and arguments, making decisions with peers: these are basic skills—prerequisite to people's development as social questioners and initiators of change. Yet few students are accustomed to independent decision-making.

Why not? The school curriculum emphasizes geography and geometry, chemistry and career ed. Where are discussions of, and experience with, democratic decision-making? The **Lawrence** role play thus becomes a possible jump-off point for exploring the nature of schooling: Why is democracy talked about but seldom practiced? What if this changed? Would offices and factories, department stores and universities welcome workers who expected a full voice in every arena of their lives? Whose interests might be threatened?

The participatory teaching methods included in this curriculum, like the **Lawrence** lesson, have a deeper aim than simply transferring information or analysis. Despair and cynicism fade when students exercise initiative and judgment. They are more likely to feel capable of making changes—both personal and social. Lectures won't convince students that they can make decisions with their peers. Nor will reading about inspiring social change make students believe that they too can take part. Listening and reading can surely help facilitate understanding; experience is what makes ideas concrete.

The Textbook of Students' Lives

A curriculum is not an educational cookbook. Students don't come guaranteed to respond identically to each curricular recipe we follow. So we're in luck. Every class offers us the opportunity to link and enrich course concepts with the diverse backgrounds of our students.

Recently, in one of our classes, we totaled the ages of students and teacher: 531 years. This combined experience is brought to every unit of study, we pointed out, and is a rich additional text.

The Power in Our Hands explores feelings and activities everyone has experienced: resistance, cooperation, competition, prejudice, powerlessness, risk taking. Throughout the lessons we've indicated points where participants might be encouraged to discuss or write about personal experiences that exemplify these and other concepts.

In the **Organic Goodie Simulation,** discussed earlier, students as workers and unemployed confront the monopolistic owner of the machine which produces all sustenance in the society. Do students feel that any effort at collective action would be betrayed? Are the owner's promises trusted? How students react to their simulated hardships and choices depends in part on the prior understandings and sensibilities they bring to the class.

A writing assignment elicits student attitudes by asking class members to describe a time in their lives when a group they were a part of acted effectively together. Alternatively, students can choose to tell of an episode when they discovered they *couldn't* count on others.

Students are generally eager to share their writing in class. This assortment of experiences becomes the material for discussion. Students begin to see how their ability to work with trust and cooperation and the attitudes that underpin this ability are shaped in part by the rest of their lives. For teachers, the discussion is an opportunity to help students make these connections; it's also informative. Learning more about our students enables us to ground future lessons in their experiences and interests, not simply in what we think in the abstract are important concepts.

Imaginative Writing. Throughout the curriculum we suggest writing topics that connect participants' lives to themes in the lessons. In **Who Makes History? (Lesson #2),** we encourage people to write poems modeled after Bertolt Brecht's "Questions of a Worker While Reading" which search out the hidden story behind a commodity or event. Some students draw on their own work lives to expose poetically the underlying reality of an efficient office or tonight's salad. Others take familiar objects and imagine the process of creation. Last year, a high school junior in one of our classes wrote a humorous but biting poem about Mr. Ruffle and his potato chip workers "who cut that extra something":

You know what it is—
into your pockets;
who go home with numb hands every day
from washing thousands of dirty potatoes in ice
*   water;*
who sit up all night picking splinters out of
*   calloused hands*
from chopping trees for paper bags that you put
*   your name on . . .*

In a later lesson, students read about C.P. Ellis, a former leader of the Ku Klux Klan who turned in his white sheets and Exalted Cyclops title when he discovered blacks made better allies than targets. After discussing Ellis's dramatic conversion to union organizer, we ask students to write about a change in *their* lives, one they hadn't before thought possible.

Asking students to reflect on their own lives more deeply roots what they've learned. From the "read-arounds," in which class members share their writing with one another, emerges a beautiful and powerful tapestry of their lives. This homespun literature becomes the experiential text for the class to analyze and admire. But a caution: while the read-arounds can build community and camaraderie, they need to be more than literary show-and-tells. The goals are to stimulate students to a dialogue with each other and with their own experiences and to reflect with greater rigor on the history, not simply to produce pretty writing.

For example, in the C.P. Ellis writing assignment just mentioned, students have written vivid accounts of a significant life change: overcoming the dread of public speaking; shaking a "crack" habit; representing co-workers in grievance proceedings; dealing with an alcoholic boyfriend. In the read-around, we urge students to listen for factors that contribute to people feeling capable—and incapable—of change. What was the relationship between external conditions, such as moving to a new school or department at work, and personal change? What influence did the act of making an important change have on students' feelings that they could move further? People put the microscope to their own experiences in order to make generalizations they can test in other contexts.

In teaching these lessons we have tried to keep alert to topics that stimulate particularly animated discussion. One year we arranged an after-school meeting between fifteen of our high school students and a researcher studying work discipline in McDonald's restaurants. The students felt good that their experiences and observations had value. More importantly, listening to one another, students saw basic similarities in their workplaces. When reminded of our paper airplane simulation and "scientific management's" breakdown of work into deskilled fragments, students had more examples from which to understand the concepts. It wasn't extra credit that kept these young workers past five in the afternoon telling stories and asking questions; it was the desire to make sense of their own experiences and the shared exhilaration of taking their work lives seriously.

Curriculum and Unions. In case it is not already apparent, we want to underscore that *The Power in Our Hands* is not a simple "pro-union" curriculum. While the lessons treat unions as vehicles for protection and improvement, they also acknowledge that unions may be at times discriminatory, at times hierarchical. Students are encouraged to be critical of all forms of domination and inequality.

Unfortunately, teaching materials by and about unions are often misleading. While depicting important struggles, they begin with too narrow an understanding of union "accomplishments." A typical curriculum will emphasize that public education, workers' compensation, unemployment insurance, social security, minimum wages, maximum hours, child labor protection, occupational safety and health regulations were fought for by organized labor. But although these reforms were indeed significant, they had their share of irony and disappointment. For example, workers' compensation is portrayed as a triumph for labor. Yet both by original design and in practice it has protected employers more than workers. Workers' comp has both stabilized employer costs and diluted corporate responsibility for worker safety and health. And it successfully diverted attention from the need for further action on occupational health and safety for half a century.

As these lessons show, the labor movement has made contributions to democratization and social justice that go well beyond lists of legislative victories. Its successes have been achieved to the extent that its own internal workings were democratic, its workplace struggles militant, and its links with other social movements deep. This is the real stuff of labor history.

Our goal here is more to probe than back-pat. Lessons like **Birth of a Rank-and-File Organizer (Lesson #9)** help students see the importance of unions. **Union Maids** and **Shutdown! (Lesson #15)** show that, even with a union, the struggle for a decent workplace and society is an ongoing process.

A Work in Progress. We first began developing these lessons in 1977. From time to time we led workshops with high school and college teachers and labor educators. In written evaluations and follow-up meetings they told us what worked and what *needed* work. This has been a fun and productive process—but one we could continue indefinitely without having a final product. While there is no such thing as a finished curriculum, we decided to stop tinkering and offer these sixteen lessons now.

Still, there are gaps. All the lessons depict work as paid labor. That leaves out housework. Nor do we deal with the steady narrowing of union activity that has resulted from legislation and court action. Issues surrounding undocumented workers in the United States—the so-called illegal aliens—are complex and deserve some sober, non-xenophobic classroom reflection. Transnational corporations now dominate our economic life, increasing the need for international coordination of unions and workers' movements. We hope you'll join us in producing new lessons that address these and other topics. (See **Evaluation,** which follows the student handouts.)

We talked with some of our students early last year about how schooling had affected all of our lives. One thoughtful young woman frowned and said, "You know, when I was little and something was wrong I wanted to change it—to make it right. But now I don't do anything because I really don't feel I can make a difference."

We don't want to work in institutions that generate despair. And we don't have to. Schools and unions are settings that can reinforce hope and enthusiasm, that can inspire a sense of justice, that can provide opportunity for democratic decision-making and participation, and that can enrich it all with knowledge.

We hope that *The Power in Our Hands* will contribute to a different vision of education, one that asserts through its content and pedagogy that yes, you can understand your life, your world—and yes, you can make change. Join with us in helping students and workers to reclaim what they should never have lost: the knowledge that they *can* make a difference.

—June 1988

UNIT I

BASIC UNDERSTANDINGS

LESSON 1

III ━━━━━━━━━━━━━━━ III

ORGANIC GOODIE SIMULATION

Can people work together to accomplish needed changes? How students answer this question will determine their attitude toward labor history. Unfortunately, many are cynical. Without challenging that cynicism, they run the risk of dismissing much of the history. This lesson lets them experience some of the pressures that lead workers to organize. Depending on what happens in class, students either glimpse the possibility of organizing and practice overcoming cynicism, or gain an experience out of which their attitudes can be directly discussed.

This first lesson lays the groundwork in two other ways. First, it is fun—at times exciting. Second, it suggests a basic skill in social analysis: learning to identify the differing, even opposing, interests of groups within society.

Goals/Objectives

1. Students will understand some of the reasons workers develop unions and other organizations.

2. Students will experience some of the techniques employers used to subvert that organizing.

Materials Needed

- One large machine-like object, e.g., a TV, a projector, or a record player.

- **Student Handout #1-A: Organic Goodie Simulation: Questions.**

- **Student Handout #1-B: Can People Act Together?**

Time Required

- One class period to "play," one-half class period to discuss.

III ━━━━━━━━━━━━━━━ III

Procedure: Day One

1. Close the door and the blinds in the class-room. Tell students to imagine that we are going to have to live in this classroom for the rest of our lives (many groans). Explain that there is no soil for farming but we are in luck because we have a machine that produces food—organic goodies. Then correct yourself and point out that actually *you* own the machine. Put the projector or whatever machine you've selected at the front of the classroom.

2. Tell students you need people to work for you producing organic goodies. Workers will receive money to buy enough food to live on—those not working will find it hard to survive. Ask for volunteers who want to work, eat, and survive. Choose only half the

Production = 11 x no. of workers

		Per day	
	Workers	*Unemployed*	*Owner*
Wages	$6 x no. workers	Nothing	Nothing
Taxes	-$1 x no. workers	+$2 x no. unemployed	-$1 x no. unemployed (see note)
Consumption	5 Organic Goodies x no. workers	2 x no. unemployed	6 Organic Goodies
Surplus	Nothing	Nothing	4 x no. workers - 6 for personal daily consumption

Example: If there were ten workers and ten unemployed, the owner would end up with 50 Goodies: 10 would go to unemployed, 6 would be consumed, leaving a remaining 34.

Note: Workers' and owner's tax needs to provide $2 to each unemployed person (taxes paid in Goodies).

class as workers. The other half will be unemployed. Sit the two opposite each other, the employed facing the unemployed.

3. Now explain the economics of your society to students. Put the "Organic Goodie Economy" chart (see above) on the board. (You might want to have the chart up earlier, covered with a map or a screen.)

Explain that five organic goodies a day are necessary to survive in a fairly healthy manner. Those receiving less, the non-workers, will gradually get sick and starve to death. Go over the chart with students: Each worker *produces* eleven (11) goodies a day. All workers are *paid* $6.00. A goodie costs $1.00. One dollar is deducted from the pay of each worker to make small welfare payments to the unemployed. So, after taxes, a worker can buy five goodies a day, enough to survive. Explain that as the owner, you naturally deserve more because it's your machine—and without your machine *everyone* would starve.

4. Show the unemployed that, as the chart indicates, they only receive $2.00 a day in welfare payments. This means they can only buy two goodies a day—they are slowly starving to death. They need work.

5. Make sure each student understands his/her position. Now the "game" begins. Your goal is to increase your profits. The way you can do this is through cutting wages.

Note: No money or goodies are actually exchanged. You might begin by telling students to imagine that a number of weeks have elapsed and then asking members of each group how they have been eating.

6. There is no "correct" order in which to proceed but here are some classroom-tested techniques:

— Ask which of the unemployed people wants to work. Offer someone $5.50 a day—less than other workers but more than the $2.00 they're getting now in welfare payments. After you have a taker, go to the workers and ask who is willing to accept $5.50. If no one is willing, fire someone and hire the unemployed person who was willing to work for that amount. Continue this procedure, trying to drive down wages.

— Anyone who mentions "union" or striking or anything disruptive should be fired immediately. Get all the workers to sign "yellow dog" contracts promising never to join a union as long as they work for you.

— You might want to hire a foreman for a little more money who will report "subversive" workers to you. Probably someone will threaten to take over your machine. When this happens, hire a policeman or two to protect it. Explain that he/she is here to protect "all our property *equally,* not just my machine."

— It's important to keep workers and unemployed from uniting in a strike—or worse, to take control of your machine. You can offer privileges to people to prevent them from seeing their interests in common—differential wages, shorter work days, perhaps even profit sharing.

— If they are successful in uniting and stopping production, you have a couple of options: (1) You can wait them out, pointing out your surplus (using the example on the chart), and how quickly they will starve; or (2) give in to their wage demands and then raise the price of organic goodies. After all,

you can justify your need for more income to meet your higher costs.

7. The game is unpredictable, and a range of things has happened in playing it. What *always* happens, however, is that people try to get themselves organized. The game ends when students have had ample opportunity to organize—successfully or otherwise. Participants may be totally demoralized—beaten down—or they may have taken over the machine. Whatever happens, and these are not the only two possibilities, make sure to continue until the game's objectives have been achieved.

8. Distribute **Student Handout #1-A: Organic Goodie Simulation: Questions** for homework. This works better than trying to discuss the game right away.

Procedure: Day Two

1. The direction of your discussion will depend on how the simulation developed. However, here are some questions that might be applicable.

— What were the major divisions set up in the role play?

— How did you feel about your role? Lucky, unlucky?

— When did you start becoming dissatisfied?

— What plans, if any, did you make to change the set-up?

— What made it difficult for you to unite with one another?

— How did you feel when I hired the police to protect "all of our property"? Why?

— What were the methods I used to try to keep people from getting together to oppose me?

— When was I successful? When unsuccessful?

— What happened to people who mentioned going on strike?

— How did you feel when I raised the price of organic goodies? Why did I say I needed this price increase? Did you accept that reason as legitimate?

— How did you feel about the foreman? Would you have liked to be the foreman? the police?

— In general, at which points were you most successful in getting together? When were you least successful?

— Were there actions that you personally considered but didn't do anything about? What kept you from acting on your ideas? (Here, try to get at students' preconceptions about whether or not people are able to stick together: Did they think that efforts to unite all workers and unemployed would eventually be betrayed? If so, explore with students what experiences they've had in groups that would make them feel skeptical about people getting together. Likewise, if students felt hopeful about the possibilities for unified action, what gave them that sense? Had past experiences convinced them that people can unite and act together?)

— As the owner, what kind of attitudes would I want you to have about your ability to work together as a unified group?

2. *Optional:* Distribute **Student Handout #1-B: Can People Act Together?** for students to complete in class or as homework. This questionnaire will allow you to continue to explore with students the origins of their sense of being able or unable to work together. Alternatively, just assign question #3 and have students write a detailed description of the time they acted in concert with others. Ask students to share their papers with the class. Possible discussion questions include:

— Does it seem that most of you are hopeful about people's abilities to work together? Where do your different views come from?

— Are there reasons why particular views of "human nature"—e.g., people are *naturally* greedy or selfish or competitive—would be encouraged by various groups in our society? Who would have wanted you to have these ideas in our **Organic Goodie Simulation?**

— What are some of the important experiences in our lives which shape our ideas about human nature (e.g., sports, school, family, work, etc.)?

— How would you reorganize these activities so that they might change our concept of "human nature"? (The goal here is to get students reflecting on "human nature" as changeable—that people may be the way they are at least partly because of the kind of society they live in.)

— Are there situations in which self-interest might best be served by uniting with others?

— From your answers, what role did outside pressures play on your ability to get together? (For example, needing to defend something people all value.)

— Can you think of a time when you accomplished something by cooperating with a group of people that you couldn't have done as well alone?

Adapted from Mike Messner, "Bubblegum and Surplus Value," *The Insurgent Sociologist* 6, no. 4 (Summer 1976): 51–56.

LESSON 2

WHO MAKES HISTORY?

The way the past is presented—or not presented—affects how people think of their own capabilities. Here, using a Bertolt Brecht poem, students begin to consider the active, creative role that workers have played in the past and their potential strength in the future.

Goals/Objectives

1. Students will be able to understand better the choices that historians make in writing history.

2. Students will develop an appreciation for the role of the ordinary people behind great historical events.

Materials Needed

- **Student Handout #2: A Worker Reads History.**

Time Required

- One class period.

Procedure

1. Have students number 1 through 10 on a sheet of paper.

2. Tell students to write a list of the ten "most famous" people in the history of the United States.

3. After they have finished, ask a few of them to share their lists. As someone suggests a name, have him/her say briefly why that person was selected.

4. Have all the students look over their lists. Ask them if they can make any generalizations about what the people they named have in common—e.g., are they mostly men? are there many presidents, athletes, explorers, or movie stars on the lists?

5. Discuss with students what type of accomplishment made each of the people on the lists famous.

— In general, what kinds of things make people famous in U.S. history?

— Are there *other* people who should get recognition for participating in the same events as the "famous people"?

— Are there other categories of people in history who have done very important things but who have not received as much credit as the "famous" people?

6. Distribute **Student Handout #2: A Worker Reads History** by Bertolt Brecht. Read the poem aloud with the class.

7. Initiate a class discussion based on the following questions:

— Who does the poet feel gets most of the credit in the history books?

— Who else does he feel are the really important people in history? What makes them important?

— Do you agree?

— Why doesn't history normally focus on workers and "common" people?

— How many working people did you include on your list?

8. Tell students that they are going to write a poem modeled after Brecht's search for the other unheralded people in history. Ask them to list a number of things in their daily lives in which the people who do or did the work are "hidden." For example, a baseball, a television program, a piece of fruit or a record album each represents a great deal of human labor, which we don't usually see. Or they might think of jobs with which they are familiar—bakeries, janitorial or secretarial work, food preparation—that are isolated from the ultimate consumers.

After students have completed their lists, have them write a poem using the themes in Brecht's "A Worker Reads History." As a prompt, you might suggest they begin with a question as Brecht does. Recall that in the **Introduction** we mentioned one student who wrote about Mr. Ruffle's workers and their relationship to the owner. You might want to share the excerpt from this student's poem with your class to provoke more ideas.

LESSON 3

III ━━━━━━━━━━━━ III

WHAT RIGHTS DO WE HAVE?

Here students begin to shake up their assumptions about labor and union history. We hope students will develop an openness—a willingness to question and reflect—that is hindered by stereotypical notions of unions and other worker organizations. The two student handouts, **What Rights Do I Have?** emphasize that studying about labor is not just "academic" but can be quite personal.

Goals/Objectives

1. Students will realize some of what they don't know about the labor movement.

2. Students will learn important background information about labor history and contemporary organized labor.

3. Students will consider rights that workers have and do not have and see that these rights are at times ambiguous.

Materials Needed

- **Student Handout #3-A: Labor Movement: What We Do and Don't Yet Know.**

- **Student Handout #3-B: What Rights Do I Have? (Part 1).**

- **Student Handout #3-C: What Rights Do I Have (Part 2).**

Time Required

- One class period.

III ━━━━━━━━━━━━ III

Procedure

1. Distribute **Student Handout #3-A: Labor Movement: What We Do and Don't Yet Know.** Go over the questions aloud and have students write their responses in class. Explain that this is not a test to be graded, but an effort to determine quickly what they know.

2. Discuss the questions one by one, drawing on the following answers:

— **1(b).** Workers have organized to protect themselves against worsening conditions ever since some people have labored for others. There are records of worker organi-

zation in the building of the pyramids. **1(c), (d),** and **(e)** all included unions, worker associations, or medieval guilds.

— **2.** A complete list would be quite long. The aim of this question is to get beyond "strike" and "negotiates wages, benefits, and working conditions" as the common answers. Some additional answers would include:

set up committees to strive for worker safety and health

promote legislation favorable to workers

represent and defend workers in disciplinary proceedings within workplaces and when workers have grievances against arbitrary authority or contract violation by management

provide a social gathering place for members or be a training ground in public speaking and running meetings and in grassroots democracy

support candidates for public office

— **3.** True. There are two major teacher unions in the United States, the National Education Association and the American Federation of Teachers. Most teachers belong to one or the other.

— **4.** This varies from workplace to workplace, often geographically. In some parts of the country, the principle of organization is by skill. There, workers may belong to *craft unions:* machinists, electrical workers, painters, etc. In other regions, all workers in a workplace are members of the same union, e.g., the United Automobile Workers, known as an *industrial union.* Supervisors are considered management and thus are generally not eligible to join a union.

— **5.** All except **(e).** The Cincinnati Redstockings were local workers who managed the team through a system of workers' control.

3. Distribute **Student Handout #3-B: What Rights Do I Have? (Part 1).** Again go over the questions aloud and have students write their responses in class. Emphasize that they are not necessarily expected to know the answers. Students should write what they think or guess the correct answer might be. An option here is to allow students to complete the handout in small groups. (After students have discussed the problems posed in the handout, you might ask for volunteers to act out the situations as improvisations.)

4. Discuss the questions one by one. An intention of this part of the lesson is for students to realize that rights they may expect or those to which they feel entitled don't necessarily exist in the workplace, or at least are not clear-cut. You may wish to have

them indicate their answers by a show of hands before discussing each. This discussion is also an opportunity to get an overview of students' own work experiences. As you discuss the questions, be sure to encourage people to use examples from their work lives. The following background information applies to the technical questions (i.e., not to the "what will you do?" and "should you . . ." questions) and is not meant as legal advice:

— **1(a).** Some states and a few cities have passed laws which say that workers, if they ask, have to be given information about the chemicals and materials they handle. There is a national law but it has many loopholes. For instance, a company does not have to inform its workers when it claims that the use of certain chemicals is a "trade secret"—a secret that the company doesn't want known to its competitors. A common practice continues to be for companies to remove or change labels or to somehow disguise the materials from the workers who are handling them. Currently, there is a national movement trying to strengthen what is called the "right to know" and the "right to act."

— **1(b).** Technically an individual may have the right to refuse work that is dangerous, as long as he or she honestly believes that the danger appears serious and immediate. In practice, companies do sometimes fire workers for refusing a direct order from a supervisor, and the process for getting a job back can be very costly and take many years.

— **2(a).** Usually, if there is a union contract with management, the worker would have the right to a hearing. Otherwise, usually not. Occasionally, groups of workers stop working and insist on an informal hearing. This is sometimes effective in making management listen.

— **2(b).** Under nearly all union contracts, the individual would be able to bring along the shop steward or a union official who knows the contract.

— **3(a).** The law continues to change. Right now, in general, the right of free speech is not considered to apply in the workplace. Handing out leaflets in the office is considered an interference with business. A worker may not have a right to post a leaflet unless there is a union and the contract says that the union can have its own bulletin board. In that case, a worker still needs union permission to put up the leaflet. On occasion workers will scatter leaflets, say, in the restrooms, in the hope that they will be seen and discussed by other workers throughout the day.

— **4(a).** This right varies from union to union. Most unions have now signed contracts that give up the right to strike except in very particular circumstances, usually when a contract expires. Even if workers feel that the contract is being violated by management, they can no longer strike but must go through complex procedures in which the decision is in the hands of judges or arbiters. Only a few unions, such as the International Woodworkers (whose members work as loggers and in lumber mills) have insisted on retaining the right to strike to prevent contract violations. In the situation described in the handout, whether the suspension or the unsafe working conditions were contract violations would depend on the contract.

5. Distribute **Student Handout #3-C: What Rights Do I Have? (Part 2)** as homework. In discussing the homework, possible questions are:

— Are there particular rights that you expect to have that you don't have or that are more limited in workplaces?

— We've seen that the same person has fewer rights inside the workplace, as a worker, than outside. Does that surprise you? If it doesn't surprise you, why not? Does it seem natural? Who benefits from these restrictions on rights?

— In some countries people have more rights in the workplace than they do here; in other countries less. Imagine a workplace in which you had all your rights as a citizen. What would be the advantages and disadvantages?

— In your job now, if you are working, are there rights you don't have that you would like?

— In your experience at work, have people ever gotten into trouble for trying to exercise rights they thought they had?

UNIT II

CHANGES IN THE WORKPLACE
"Scientific Management"

LESSON 4

III ════════════════════ III

PAPER AIRPLANE SIMULATION

There were major changes around the turn of the century in how workplaces were structured and work organized. These changes occurred at different paces in different industries and, in modified form, continue today. Systematizing and justifying the new management practices, Frederick Winslow Taylor contributed his name to our language. "Taylorism," according to the dictionary, means "scientific management."

    With the help of paper airplanes and chocolate, this lesson shows students a key aspect of the changes occurring at the workplace: the attempted capture of workers' skill and knowledge by management.

Goals/Objectives

1. Students will gain a first-hand appreciation of the impact that "scientific management" had on the lives of working people.

2. Students will acquire a theoretical understanding of the stages of Frederick Taylor's scientific management.

Materials Needed

- 35 sheets of 8½″ by 11″ scratch paper.

- A large chocolate bar.

- A camera or reasonable facsimile.

- **Student Handout #4: Frederick W. Taylor: Taylorisms.**

Time Required

- One and one-half to two class periods.

III ════════════════════ III

Procedure

1. Ask for volunteers who have two things in common: each has to be able to make a paper airplane that can fly, and each must like chocolate. (There's never any difficulty finding volunteers!)

2. Choose five volunteers (four in a smaller class) and send them out of the room. Close the door.

3. Explain to the rest of the class that you are a factory owner. Your factory produces paper airplanes. As the owner, you own the building in which the workers labor, you own the materials with which they labor, and you own the finished product. Ask students what you *don't* own. Answer: the workers' *knowledge*—they are the ones who know *how* to produce the planes. Explain that you are going to acquire this knowledge from the workers without them realizing it.

    Ask for a volunteer to "photograph" the workers as they produce the planes. This volunteer should receive a small piece of chocolate in payment after he/she completes the job.

4. Bring the five volunteers back into the classroom. Explain that they are all workers in your paper airplane factory. You are going to have a contest. The first person to complete five airplanes that *fly* will be declared the winner and be given a large part of a chocolate bar.

5. Seat them at desks in front of the class. Give each one two sheets of paper for practice. They should make the practice planes and fly them. (Emphasize that only the "contestants" may fly planes. Unless you enforce this, the result will be chaos.)

6. After they've practiced, give them each five sheets of paper. Get two more volunteers—one to judge when the planes are complete, the other to serve as the timekeeper. Explain to the workers that each should continue making planes until all five planes are finished.

7. Have them begin. The timekeeper should record when each of them completes all his/her planes. Make sure that throughout this process, the photographer is busy recording all the different methods of plane construction.

8. When all the workers have finished their planes, ask the first person who finished to throw all five of his/her planes. If the judge determines them "airworthy," this person is declared the winner and given the chocolate—if not, continue to the next fastest person until a winner is determined. Award smaller pieces of chocolate to the timekeeper, photographer, and judge.

9. Explain to the workers that before the contest you (the teacher) owned the factory, the raw materials—paper—and the finished products—paper airplanes—but they owned the knowledge of how those planes were produced. This fact caused you, as the owner, some problems: workers could demand high wages for their skills and, in the event of a strike, they could successfully halt production by withholding their skilled labor.

"Let's see how our little contest is going to change the rules of the game." (Keep the workers at the "workplace," in other words, seated as they are in front of the class.)

10. On the board or overhead projector make two columns: one labeled "owner" and one "worker." In a discussion question/answer format with students, complete the "owner" column, then move on to the "worker" column (see next page, **Paper Airplane Discussion**). When you get to the point in the discussion where you talk about who you could hire to do the work, emphasize this point by firing skilled workers, sending them back to their seats, and hiring other students as unskilled workers: immigrants, children, women, etc.

11. Tell students that this process, called "scientific management," was developed by Frederick W. Taylor.

12. Distribute **Student Handout #4: Frederick W. Taylor: Taylorisms.** Review this sheet with students. Have students save these "Taylorisms" for a later lesson. (*Note:* The quotes in this reading are from Taylor himself. Occasionally two separate quotes have been joined to form a more complete idea. No meanings have been changed. *Source:* Harry Braverman, *Labor and Monopoly Capital* [New York: Monthly Review Press, 1974], pp. 85–123.)

13. Assign homework: (a) Write a short essay explaining why many managers and owners would probably appreciate Taylor's scientific management techniques and why many skilled workers probably would object to them. (b) What are some of the techniques workers might use to resist putting scientific management into effect?

PAPER AIRPLANE DISCUSSION

Owner

What knowledge do I now have that I didn't have before?

Step-by-step knowledge of actual process of production.

Time required at each step of the process.

What can I do now that I have acquired this new knowledge by taking pictures of the production process?

Could enforce fastest speed as the norm for all workers.

Could force all workers to produce planes in the same manner as the fastest worker.

What can I change about the process of making paper airplanes? (Remember, my goal is to cut costs and increase profits.)

Can fire highly paid skilled workers and hire cheaper unskilled workers.

These new workers could be assigned one minute task, say a particular fold.

Workers would do one thing over and over, passing each part on to the next worker, assembly-line fashion.

Now that I have the knowledge of how planes are produced, whom could I get to be my unskilled workers?

Women, children, immigrants, etc.

If there had been a union at the paper airplane factory, what might happen to it?

Workers building one small part of airplane are more easily replaced. Consequently, strikes would be less effective.

Workers

What will be some of the consequences of the changes in production for the workers if the same people are kept on? How will the character of their work be changed?

Paid less.

More boring work—doing one thing over and over again.

More watched and regulated by their employer.

Work greatly speeded up.

How might workers feel differently about the process of making paper airplanes?

Less pride—they no longer make the entire planes themselves.

Less satisfaction or interest as there is no *thought* involved in the work—workers have been stripped of all brainwork.

Less independent and powerful—more dependent on owners for instructions. (No longer have the same ability to stop production as skilled workers.)

How could these changes affect family life or personal relations?

Less fulfilled, workers could take out their frustrations on family.

Paid less, a family's standard of living would decline.

On the job, workers will not know each other as well with managers able to enforce stricter rules.

With older, slower workers fired and younger, stronger workers hired, resentments would be created, making it hard to keep a union together.

LESSON 5

FREE TO THINK, TALK, LISTEN, OR SING

In **Paper Airplane,** students "saw" some of the key turn-of-the-century workplace changes, which continue to affect workers. Here they explore some of the historical background. The reading in this lesson recounts how new technologies and workplace structures affected the most intimate aspects of people's lives. Often, workers' demands made in negotiations don't fully reveal the human consequences of work. Even when the call is for higher wages, the underlying grievances may be much deeper.

Goals/Objectives

1. Students will appreciate how changes in work organization affected the working conditions in factories in the United States.

2. Students will recognize how changes in people's work lives have consequences for their home and family lives as well.

Materials Needed

- **Student Handout #5: Free to Think, Talk, Listen, or Sing** (from Milton Meltzer, *Bread and Roses* [New York: Vintage, 1973]).

Time Required

- One class period and homework.

Procedure

1. Depending on the skill level of the class, either assign the reading as homework or read the selection aloud.

2. The writing assignment at the conclusion of **Student Handout #5: Free to Think, Talk, Listen, or Sing** should be given as homework.
   Note: Encourage students to be especially creative in their completion of the homework. In choice #2, you might suggest that they do this as an illustrated poster or a handbill. Urge them to imagine a particular shoe factory in Massachusetts and to make the complaints and demands very specific. We've received wonderfully imaginative and moving pieces of work from this assignment.

3. Some discussion questions could include:

— One worker stated that the subdivision of labor into smaller and smaller parts had a "very demoralizing effect upon the mind" of the worker. What does the writer mean by "demoralizing"? What are some examples?

— One mill superintendent described switching from the older technique of mule spinning—requiring highly skilled workers—to the newer method of ring spinning. According to the superintendent, was it just the desire for increased efficiency in production that led to this shift? What motivated this switch in spinning methods?

— A Mr. Eaton explained that with the new changes in the shoe industry, a worker might operate a machine that nailed the heels on 4,800 shoes in a single day. Have you ever done repetitive work like that—in fast food, picking in the fields, in a factory? How did it make you feel? How did it affect your thinking? Did you do anything to prevent yourself from feeling like a machine?

— How might the changes in the shoe industry affect someone who had been used to making the whole shoe?

— What happened to the wages of workers as industrial work became increasingly fragmented—divided into narrower tasks?

— According to the quotes from Mr. Eaton and Samuel Gompers, what was it about the older organization of production that made it easier for workers to develop themselves intellectually? In what ways could a more thoughtful and critical working class be threatening to the owners with their new production methods?

— Look at the cost-of-living sheet, taken from the *Printer* of August 1864, for a family of six. The paper points out that the average wage for a printer was $16 a week, with other trades paid as little as $6 or even $3. If you were having to make do on $16 a week, which items would you eliminate from the list of food and other family expenses? What does the list not include that you would want for your family? What choices would your family be faced with?

— Ira Stewart, a machinist writing in *Fincher's Trades' Review,* was upset at more than the low wages of workers. What did he fear was happening to American workers?

LESSON 6

MODERN TIMES

This is a graphic and entertaining illustration of the two previous lessons. **Paper Airplane** demonstrated the transition to increased management control and the lessened skill levels and less meaningful work that followed. **Free to Think, Talk, Listen, or Sing** gave the historical background. Here students see the workplace consequences. Although the movie is a caricature, it highlights people's real experiences. Notice the absence of black workers, who will shortly become an important force in unionizing heavy industry.

Goals/Objectives

1. Students will explore a range of ways working people were affected by industrialization.

2. Students will reflect on the role of management in an industrial enterprise.

3. Students will enjoy watching part of a Charlie Chaplin film.

Materials Needed

- Reel one of *Modern Times*. Public libraries often have copies of this film. It is also widely available for rent in video stores. The film is also available for purchase on videotape from:

  Zenger Video
  10,000 Culver Blvd., Dept. 9A
  P.O. Box 802
  Culver City, CA 90232-0802

Time Required

- One class period.

Procedure

1. Prepare students for viewing the film by providing a little background:

   Modern Times was filmed in 1935, during the Depression, and released in 1936. It was the last major movie of the silent film era. This film was also the last appearance of the Little Tramp, the character Charlie Chaplin played in a number of his movies. The Little Tramp always stood almost outside society, making his own individual way down the road. Chaplin reportedly got the idea for the film when he was told about automobile assembly-line workers in De-troit who were going crazy on their jobs. *Modern Times* was banned in fascist Germany and Italy.

2. Show the film. The running time for part one is 19 minutes. If video format is used, stop the film as the Little Tramp is carted off to the mental hospital.

3. After the showing, ask students to list all the effects of factory work on the workers in the film.

4. Have students use their lists as a basis for discussing the following questions:

— What are the conditions of work for the men in Chaplin's factory?

— What do you think it would be like to work in Chaplin's factory?

— What does the boss in the factory do?

— What are his main concerns?

— How does he treat the workers?

— Do you think the boss has studied the techniques of scientific management? (You might briefly review the stages of scientific management: (1) Managers observe and record the process of work. (2) The process is redesigned by management to facilitate control. (3) Workers' tasks are reassigned based on management's new designs.)

— Can you cite some examples? (Possible answers include: use of TV cameras, of the assembly line—management's ability to control its speed, willingness to try out automatic eating machine.)

— Why does the boss bring in the eating machine? Why does he decide to get rid of it? Is it because the machine might have a negative effect on the workers?

— How does the boss relate to the foreman?

— What does the foreman do?

— What is the foreman's attitude toward the workers in the factory?

— How do you think the assembly line affects the workers? How does it affect Chaplin?

— What makes you realize the other men, as well as Chaplin, are affected psychologically? (Remember how Chaplin stopped the men from chasing him when he was squirting them with oil.)

— Why does Chaplin go crazy?

— What goal do you think Chaplin had in mind when he made this film?

— Based on your knowledge of Nazi Germany and Mussolini's Italy, do you have any idea why they would have banned this movie?

5. Homework: after the film discussion, have students write an "interior monologue" from Chaplin's point of view after he is taken to the mental hospital. Students should write in a first-person format: What is Chaplin thinking? Is he worried? Is he angry? Does he have an understanding of what caused his problems?

LESSON 7

"TAYLORIZING" BURGERS: A FANTASY

This unit concludes by drawing on the three previous lessons for a look at the present. Since working in a fast-food restaurant is a common high school job, students here reflect on "scientific management" with reference to their own experiences. **Paper Airplane** and **Free to Think, Talk, Listen, or Sing** explored reasons for the changes in workplaces. Students now may recognize that work could be organized differently than it presently is. That realization is an important aspect of not simply accepting their surroundings as natural or inevitable. The knowledge that things could be different is as crucial for understanding history as it is for feeling capable of taking meaningful action.

While students may find the work conditions described in this lesson desirable, they should be encouraged to be critical of these as well. Job rotation, for instance, may not be sufficient to solve the problems highlighted by the previous lessons. All of these arrangements, however, have been common in recent memory. Having one worker read aloud while the others worked, for example, was a contract provision won in the cigar-making industry.

Goals/Objectives

1. Students will demonstrate a working knowledge of the principles of "scientific management" and recognize that alternative principles can also be applied in a workplace.

2. Students will further develop abilities to work cooperatively in small group settings.

Materials Needed

- **Student Handout #7-A: "Taylorizing" Burgers: A Fantasy.**

- **Student Handout #7-B: Confessions of a French-Fry Champion.**

Time Required

- One and one-half class periods.

Procedure

1. Read aloud with students **Student Handout #7-A: "Taylorizing" Burgers: A Fantasy.**

2. Discuss with students the work organization in the All-American Deluxe Hamburger Shoppe:

— Taylor calls this work process extremely "inefficient." When he uses this word, he means that it is not efficient in accomplishing a particular goal. In what ways is the Hamburger Shoppe not "efficient"? Who benefits from Taylor's brand of efficiency?

— In what ways is this work process "efficient"? Is the workplace efficient in terms of producing a stimulating work environment for the employees? In terms of producing healthy food? etc.

3. Tell students that their task is to complete the advice Taylor might give to the owner. Have students refer to **Student Handout**

#4: Frederick W. Taylor: Taylorisms (from the **Paper Airplane** lesson). Review these as a class so that everyone will be prepared to come up with some "good" advice. You might also remind students of some of the ideas the class proposed for restructuring the process of making paper airplanes.

4. Divide the class into groups of three. Have these groups give advice to the owner in the four different categories indicated at the end of the story.

5. Bring students into a circle. Ask for volunteers to read advice to the owner. Be sure students relate their suggestions to Taylor's principles of scientific management.

Compare the changes in their new restaurant with any others they might be familiar with, especially those such as Burger King, McDonald's, Kentucky Fried Chicken, etc. Make efforts to draw out students' work experiences at these types of restaurants.

Talk especially about how the changes students proposed would affect workers: their relationships with one another, the kinds of skills they would or would not learn, how they would feel about their work, etc.

Note: This lesson might provide an opportunity for students to research different workplaces and how the structure of a workplace helps determine the skills and attitudes workers acquire. Students questioning the structure of their own and friends' work situations will help them understand these environments as shaped by people with particular interests rather than as part of a natural order.

We've included an optional **Student Handout #7-B: Confessions of a French-Fry Champion.** This story describes the Taylorized work environment at a McDonald's restaurant. It's a humorous first-person account of one teenager's job conditions, and can be used as a model to encourage students to write similar analyses of their workplaces. While **Confessions** is set in a fast-food restaurant, the writer's attention to detail in recounting the highly specialized work procedures and how those affect the worker is a useful example for people examining any number of jobs.

UNIT III

DEFEATS, VICTORIES, CHALLENGES

LESSON 8

III ━━━━━━━━━━━━━━━ III

THE HOMESTEAD STRIKE

In the last unit students looked primarily at management initiatives. Now we turn to workers' responses. Central to those responses is the possibility of solidarity among workers of very different backgrounds and at different levels in the workplace hierarchy. In **Organic Goodie Simulation,** your students may have been skeptical about the possibility of people genuinely working together when at least their short-term interests appeared in conflict. **Homestead** is a historical test case—and maybe revelation—for such skepticism.

Students begin to explore in this lesson some of the themes that will appear in subsequent lessons: different types of unions; the role of government intervention; new capital formations that stimulated industry-wide organization among workers.

Goals/Objectives

1. Students will explore some of the reasons for, and results of, industrial reorganization in the late 1800s.

2. Students will gain an understanding of the conflicts between, and common interests among, skilled and unskilled workers at the turn of the century.

3. Students will develop an appreciation of some of the difficulties associated with early craft unionism.

4. Students will explore the conflict between immigrants and native-born Americans at the turn of the century.

Materials Needed

● **Student Handout #8-A: The Homestead Strike.**

● **Student Handout #8-B: Skilled Worker; #8-C: Unskilled Worker.**

● **Secret Student Handout: Company Spy.**

● **Student Handout #8-D: Homestead Strike: The Outcome.**

Time Required

● Approximately one class period and two homework assignments.

III ━━━━━━━━━━━━━━━ III

Procedure

1. Distribute **Student Handout #8-A: The Homestead Strike.** Assign students to complete the reading and answer the accompanying questions for homework.

2. Next day, review the homework questions. A successful role play requires that stu-

dents thoroughly understand the issues in the reading.

3. Divide the class into two groups, skilled and unskilled, roughly proportional in size to those two groups at Homestead: 20 percent skilled, 80 percent unskilled. Give each stu-

dent a copy of the appropriate role.

4. Choose an articulate student in the unskilled workers group and inconspicuously give this person the **Company Spy** role.

5. Have the two groups, skilled and unskilled, meet separately for about ten minutes to discuss and answer their respective questions. (The spy should meet with the unskilled.) Students may answer the questions verbally or in writing. Stress to both groups that they *may* choose to reach consensus as a group on their opinions, but that they do not *have* to. As long as students act consistently with their roles, individuals may disagree.

6. Call the "mass meeting" to order. Explain that you are a retired worker, respected by skilled and unskilled alike, whom the union has asked to chair the meeting. Your role during the meeting will be to ask questions and ensure that each side presents its ideas. (See **Homestead Strike: Notes to the Teacher** for a list of some arguments that should come out of the discussion.)

7. At the end of the meeting, after everyone has had a chance to express his/her opinions, have all the workers vote on whether or not to support the strike.

8. Ask students to step out of their roles to discuss the role play. The following questions could be used as the basis for discussion, or for a writing assignment:

— How did you feel toward members of the other group during the meeting?

— Did people play their roles realistically?

— *Unskilled:* What led you to reach your decision? Which arguments were most convincing? What might have made you decide differently?

— *Skilled:* How well were you able to predict the unskilled workers' doubts? Do you feel that you spoke to these doubts adequately? How would you explain your success or lack of success in convincing people? What else could you have done?

— What role did (name of the spy) play in the discussion? Did you suspect that he/she was being paid by the company? Why or why not?

— If this were a real situation, what do you think would have happened after the meeting? Why?

— Thinking over the role play as a whole, what would you say made it hard to get together? What made it easy?

9. Distribute **Student Handout #8-D: Homestead Strike: The Outcome.** Students should complete the reading and answer the questions for homework.

   After students have completed the homework, ask for their reactions to the agreement of the unskilled to support the skilled workers. Often, students in the role play will not be able to unite or will have serious problems arriving at an agreement. If this has been the case, explore with students why they had more difficulty than the Homestead workers had in real life. Could it have anything to do with students' sense of people's ability to stick together even when they have important differences, as we examined in the **Organic Goodie** lesson? What were the important factors uniting the skilled and unskilled workers at Homestead?

NOTES TO THE TEACHER
HOMESTEAD STRIKE

Arguments in favor of the unskilled supporting the strike

1. Changes planned by management might affect unskilled as well:

— *their* wages, pegged to those of the skilled workers, would probably also be cut

— work more monotonous

— less autonomy, ability to regulate pace, make any decisions

— speed-up

— longer hours

— layoffs, as productivity increases

— worsened safety conditions with speed-up

2. Only chance of defeating these plans lies in unity.

3. If the strike should fail, the unskilled would lose all hope of becoming skilled workers.

4. If the unskilled support the strike, they may be able to count on the skilled for help in the future.

5. If strike is defeated, unskilled lose any chance of organizing or of joining union in the days ahead. Thus they give up hope of improved conditions and protection and the means for securing more control over working conditions.

6. To scab would mean bitterness, possibly even violence from union members.

7. The solidarity between skilled and unskilled built during the course of the strike could provide the basis for a unified movement for changes that would be in all their interests.

Arguments against unskilled supporting the strike

1. Unskilled have much to lose if they strike:

— easier to replace than skilled workers

— could be evicted from company houses

— could be blacklisted

— could suffer violence at hands of company

2. Gains from striking unclear:

— strike could fail

— skilled could sell them out

— skilled have never looked out for unskilled in past, so why do so now

— skilled use ethnic slurs against them

3. Changes in the work process might even create more jobs for them—if they were content to remain unskilled.

SECRET STUDENT HANDOUT
COMPANY SPY

You have a special role. You are not only an unskilled worker, but also a company spy. Besides gathering information, you have been instructed (and well paid) to do whatever you can to sabotage the strike by setting the groups against each other and by trying to convince the unskilled *not* to support the strikers.

Do *not* reveal your role unless you are willing to give up your handsome paycheck.

LESSON 9

BIRTH OF A RANK-AND-FILE ORGANIZER

How did workers respond to workplace changes introduced by management? Their strongest response was the formation of unions. In this lesson, students read about the spontaneous organizing of men and women in a Chicago glove-making factory. As participants, students are called upon to assess the importance of union recognition: should they continue to strike for their union even if all other demands have been satisfied?

Goals/Objectives

1. Students will become aware of a range of causes for strikes.

2. Students will empathize with the problems of workers on strike.

3. Students will weigh the importance of the union shop in relation to no union organization.

Materials Needed

● **Student Handout #9-A: Birth of a Rank-and-File Organizer.**

● **Student Handout #9-B: Birth of a Rank-and-File Organizer: The Conclusion.** (Student copies of this reading are optional.)

Time Required

● One class period, plus part of a second period.

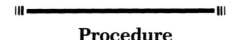

Procedure

1. In class, read aloud **Student Handout #9-A: Birth of a Rank-and-File Organizer.** The story is told by Agnes Nestor, who works in a glove-making factory in Chicago. Though at first she enjoys her work, changes introduced by management eventually lead to a strike. The workers have a number of demands, one of which is that the company will agree to a union shop, including recognition of the union and a willingness to bargain collectively.

The students' copy of the story ends with management sending individual letters to the strikers agreeing to meet their demands.

However, the company's letter does not even mention the demand for a union shop.

2. Stop reading at the close of the students' copy. At this point the women must decide whether to accept management's offer and return to work, or to continue the strike and hold out for a union shop.

3. Ask students to finish the story. They should continue to write from Agnes Nestor's point of view, describing how they think the women would or *should* have responded to the company. Their task is to bring the strike to a conclusion. While we're reluctant to set a specific length for an assignment such as this, emphasize to students that there are hard choices for the women to make and a good deal of discussion among them will probably take place. Student stories should reflect the difficult nature of the decision.

Suggest or brainstorm some possible events that could have occurred: the strikers get together in each others' homes to discuss their response; a large meeting is held to air different views; some women return to work as others continue on strike. Encourage students to write the dialogue between strikers and to get inside Nestor's thoughts and feelings.

Alternatively, have students write an interior monologue from Agnes Nestor's point of view. Students should imagine they are Nestor and write her thoughts and feelings from a first-person perspective: What worries or doubts does she have? Should the women go back to work? How important is the union shop? etc.

4. In class, encourage people to read their stories aloud. Discuss the merits of the various conclusions that the students chose.

Some questions to consider while discussing the different conclusions:

— Why do the foremen act as they do? Is it merely personal pettiness or are they attempting to heighten divisiveness and/or maintain their own control?

— Why might the union shop be *the* most important demand of the strikers?

— What could happen to the workers if they returned to work without the union shop?

— The strike has gone on for almost two weeks. Can you think of any problems the strikers might experience if they refuse the company's offer?

— What are some strategies the company could use if the workers refuse to return?

— If the union shop is won by the workers, will they all live happily ever after? What problems will they still have to face? How might the employer try to reverse their gains? What divisions among the workers in the glove factory will still need to be overcome?

5. As students share their stories and monologues, we are often struck by the dramatically different outcomes of the strike people anticipate. Some versions end in utter disarray and despair; others portray triumphant conclusions with airtight solidarity. In discussion, we encourage students to reflect on *why* they chose such different endings— what in their *own* experiences made them more or less hopeful?

6. After the discussion, read aloud the actual ending (**Birth of a Rank-and-File Organizer: The Conclusion**). Compare the results of the strike to the endings the students projected.

LESSON 10

Ⅲ─────────────────Ⅲ

LAWRENCE, 1912: THE SINGING STRIKE

Unions can have quite different objectives and modes of organization than those of the unions that predominate now. In **Lawrence, 1912,** students contrast the American Federation of Labor and the Industrial Workers of the World.

In **"Taylorizing" Burgers,** students played "scientific managers." Here they act as, and empathize with, union organizers. They also engage in one of the first and most inspirational major victories for U.S. labor.

Birth of a Rank-and-File Organizer shows that the newly found workplace solidarity had to be institutionalized in order to be sustained. Here, students take this insight further, exploring some of the practicalities of building cooperation and organization and avoiding some of the pitfalls, such as authoritarian leadership. This lesson broadens students' sense of what workers can and do fight for beyond wages and benefits, beyond "bread."

Goals/Objectives

1. Students will become familiar with different understandings of the function and purpose of labor unions.

2. Students will see relationships between these different conceptions of unions and the actual organizations that were built.

3. Students will learn about some of the practicalities of labor organizing.

4. Students will become aware of their strengths and weaknesses in collective decision-making.

Materials Needed

- **Student Handout #10-A: You Are in the IWW.**

- **Student Handout #10-B: Lawrence, 1912—Part 1: The Strike Is On!**

- **Student Handout #10-C: Lawrence Problem Solving #1: Getting Organized.**

- **Student Handout #10-D: Lawrence, 1912—Part 2: Unity in Diversity** (student copies optional).

- **Student Handout #10-E: "Bread and Roses."**

- **Student Handout #10-F: Lawrence Problem Solving #2: Can We Win?**

- **Student Handout #10-G: Lawrence, 1912—Part 3: The Outcome.**

Time Required

- Seven to ten class periods (and worth it!). Even more than in most lessons, the number of days and how much you get through each day will depend on how students respond and which of the recommended options you select.

‖ ▬▬▬▬▬▬▬▬▬▬▬▬▬▬▬▬ ‖

Procedure: Day 1

1. Distribute **Student Handout #10-A: You Are in the IWW.** Explain to students that they will be involved in a long role play in which each of them will become a member of the Industrial Workers of the World—the IWW. Therefore, it will be important that they fully understand their roles. Tell students that you will put them in small groups so that they can help one another and so that you can better assist them in their work. Encourage students to complete the AFL/IWW comparisons in as much detail as possible.

After they understand the assignment, form the groups and ask students to read the roles and answer the questions. This should take the rest of the period.

Procedure: Day 2

1. Discuss with students the IWW roles and the questions from the previous day:

— What big changes have occurred in the workplace?

— How were tools owned before? How are they owned in the workplace now?

— What is a craft union?

— What change has taken place in the ownership of industry?

— How do all these changes affect the ability of unions to bargain for their members?

— What kinds of workers does the AFL try to organize?

— Whom does the IWW try to organize?

— Remind them of Big Bill Haywood's metaphor of the hand from the reading. What was the point of this demonstration by Haywood? How is the IWW able to bring the separate fingers together into a fist? Is it simply that the IWW doesn't divide people by craft, as the AFL does? How is the kind of education and involvement encouraged of IWW members important in uniting workers?

— What do IWW members think the goal of a union should be? (What kind of society do you want to create?)

— Why do you sing together?

— When management or police want to talk with the IWW and say they'll speak only with the one or two leaders, how would you respond? (The usual IWW reply was "We are all leaders. You'll have to talk with all of us.")

— Have students recall what occurred in the **Organic Goodie** role play. Ask how they answered questions 2 and 3 on the **You Are in the IWW** handout, which dealt with the reactions of the AFL and IWW toward the actions students took.

2. To clarify the reading up to this point, suggest that students imagine an industry producing a familiar product, such as shoes. Have them picture a number of shoe factories, set in different geographical locations. Ask how many owners there might have been at an earlier time. By 1912, if the number of factories stayed the same, would we expect more, fewer, or the same number of owners? If there had been a union in one of the factories at an earlier time, and the same union existed in 1912, how would the concentration of ownership have affected it? (It could be placed in competition with other workers in other factories of the same owner. Now if it went on strike, the company still could obtain the same products or even increase production at its other factories.) Inside the factory, how have tools changed? Are there different kinds of workers? What would the IWW do about the changes in working conditions?

3. Tell students to keep the handout for reference. This will be their role for the next few classes.

4. Remind students they are IWW members and tell them you are going to interview them about their ideas. Play this part with a contentious attitude, acting more as "devil's advocate" than as neutral questioner. (To introduce this, tell students that you are in the AFL and have some opinions about the IWW.) Pose these questions as challenges:

— Why do you think women can be organized?

— How can immigrant groups that don't even speak the same language get together in a union?

— What makes you think that the whole society can be changed? What makes you believe that lowly unskilled workers are in any position to change society?

— If you don't recognize the right of owners to own, how could anything even be produced? Who would get everybody organized and working?

— If everybody in the IWW is a leader, if members are active all the time, what need is there for union officials? What would they do?

— If the AFL is so bad, why does it have so many more members around the country than the IWW?

Procedure: Day 3

1. Explain to students that as IWW members, they are going to be part of an important strike involving thousands of people. Their goal is both to build a strike that can win and to build a union in line with the IWW principles they discussed in previous sessions. Before talking about the specific strike, we need to discuss how to accomplish our larger, long-term goals: how to build a union where all the members are leaders as well as organizers for social change.

2. Write on the blackboard or sheet of butcher paper the following quote from Eugene V. Debs, a founder of the IWW:

Too long have the workers of the world waited for some Moses to lead them out of bondage. He has not come; he never will come. I would not lead you out if I could; for if you could be led out, you could be led back again. I would have you make up your minds that there is nothing that you cannot do for yourselves.

Read this aloud with the class. Ask them:

— What would people have to believe about themselves in order to accept that paragraph? What attitudes would organizers need to develop and help others develop? (Some possible answers include: that we can act on our convictions; that we are able to join with others; that our actions together can make a difference.)

List student contributions on the board.

3. Ask the class:

— If you, as IWW members, are really serious about building a society run by all the workers, and not just the owners, what skills would you have to develop in yourselves and in new members? (Some possible answers include: the ability to speak well publicly or to write or otherwise reach people persuasively; the ability to conduct meetings; the ability to analyze a particular situation and to think of appropriate tactics.)

Again, list student contributions on the board.

4. Distribute **Student Handout #10-B: Lawrence, 1912—Part 1** and **Student Handout #10-C: Lawrence Problem Solving #1.** If there is time, begin the selection in class. Homework is to complete the reading and to jot down ideas for each of the questions in the problem solving.

Procedure: Day 4

1. Review **Student Handout #10-C** with students, focusing on the background to the strike:

— Why did the strike occur? Besides the immediate events, the speed-up and pay cut, what about working and living conditions was important in the decision to strike?

— What obstacles face IWW organizers attempting to build a unified strike? What divisions might exist within the workforce or community? What attitudes toward authority? Is the lack of tradition in organizing this kind of workforce an obstacle?

— Why did the AFL act as it did?

2. Remind students that they are IWW members, planning and leading what they can now see as a very complicated struggle. Once again, their goal is not simply to win the strike (though that's important), but to build a union along the principles of the IWW. The first problems they will have to face are those on **Student Handout #10-C: Lawrence Problem Solving #1.** Even before that, however, they'll have to decide on the *process* they'll use in solving the problems.

3. Seat the students in a circle so that they can talk to one another more easily. Explain that because theirs is a democratic union and because they believe in equality, no one will be around to *tell* them what to do. In the IWW, not only would they not allow a single individual to make decisions for everyone else, but they would try to encourage the broadest possible participation. The strike will succeed only because they are able to make it succeed—together. Therefore, you (the teacher) will play no role in their discussions. Once their strike meeting begins, you will be just an observer. It will be up to the entire class to decide how to make decisions and what those decisions should be.

4. Once they understand that you won't assist with their deliberations, you may want to discuss with them some of the ways they can reach decisions. For example, they could select a chairperson who would then call on individuals to speak and propose when votes might be taken. Perhaps they will want to avoid leaders entirely—students might raise hands, with the last person to speak calling on the next speaker and so on. Or a rotating chairperson might be decided upon—one chair per question, for example. The teacher's job is merely to help the students to make their own decisions. This is an essential part of the role play.

5. Tell students that the questions in the handout were genuine concerns in the actual strike. (It's not important that students arrive at the historically accurate answers—they'll be able to find those answers in their homework reading. What is important is that they discuss the questions in terms of the IWW principles and goals.) Remind them to answer each of the questions as fully as possible. Tell them you will be available only if they have difficulty understanding any of the six questions.

6. Allow them to begin their meeting. Because students are not used to having to organize a discussion without the assistance of an authority figure, they may find it rough going at first. That's fine. Let them discover their own problems and solutions. Intervene only if you sense they are hopelessly frustrated, and then only to help them establish a clear decision-making process. As the meeting progresses, take notes on both their decision-making successes and failures and on the different ideas and arguments that are raised in answering the questions.

7. At the conclusion of the strike meeting, ask students to write evaluations of their decisions and of the process that brought them to those decisions. Taking this break for reflection sometimes enables a class to discuss experiences a little more thoughtfully.

Procedure: Day 5 (or so)

1. Tell students that it's time to find out how the strikers actually solved the problems with which the class has been dealing. Tell them to listen closely to compare the real decisions with the ones they had reached.

2. Read aloud **Student Handout #10-D: Lawrence, 1912—Part 2.**

3. Review the six questions of **Lawrence Problem Solving #1** one by one. Ask the students to recall from their reading what actually happened. Then have them compare it, in light of the IWW's goals, to their own decisions in the previous class.

4. Discussion of the students' *process* of decision-making should follow discussion of their decisions. There will be an opportunity for a fuller discussion later in the lesson. At this point, the questions are simply:

— What went wrong in the discussion. Why?

— What was good about the discussion?

— How might the organizational meeting have gone better? Try to reach some decisions here because the class will soon be in the same group decision-making process.

5. (*Optional*) For a written homework assignment, encourage students to produce either a strike leaflet directed toward any individuals still crossing picket lines, or an appeal for aid to workers in other cities. In each case the leaflet or appeal should urge support for the strike and offer suggestions for how others could help. Encourage students to be both eloquent and artistic in their appeals.

You might suggest that students complete their "leaflets" in the form of songs. One year a number of our students wrote and performed songs based on melodies from contemporary music. While not strictly historically accurate, these efforts added drama and spirit to the lesson.

Procedure: Day 6

1. Let students keep their homework for the moment. Explain that this was known as the "singing strike." Distribute **Student Handout #10-E: "Bread and Roses"** and read it together.

2. Discuss with students the significance of singing on the picket lines and at meetings. Reporters at the time noted the way singing unified the various nationalities and lifted spirits in the difficult conditions of the strike. Even when the languages were different, the melodies were familiar. Songs also helped remind workers of the strike's broader goals.

3. If you've been able to find a recording of "Bread and Roses," play it for the class and/or ask the class to join the singing. Discuss the questions that accompany the song on the handout. In particular, what are the issues and demands other than wages for which people struggle? Are working conditions part of "bread" or "roses" or both? What grievances might underlie a demand for higher wages (e.g., desired changes in living conditions or difficulties in accomplishing other needed changes at work)?

4. If you decided to assign the optional homework, have students read or perform what they produced. Ask for additional suggestions that could make for an effective appeal to other workers or could communicate the broader objectives of the strike.

5. (*Optional:* There are important questions about the mechanics of running a strike that have not yet been explored with students. However, if pressed for time this next segment of the lesson can be skipped—go to instruction #7.)

   Tell the students that it's time to be concerned with the nitty-gritty workings of conducting a strike. Ask them:

— Now that we have a basic, decision-making, organizational structure in place, what are the different kinds of tasks that need to be done? (A different way of asking the same question might be: what are the subcommittees we need to create?)

   Write student suggestions on the board. The objective here is to recognize the tasks rather than to discuss in detail how to carry them out. Here are a few additional questions that suggest specific tasks:

— Since people aren't working now, they have no income. How will they eat?

— There is a lot of pressure on people. How can we maintain morale?

— How can we encourage support for our strike in the community and even outside of Lawrence?

— We can't expect the newspapers to be sympathetic. How can we get our side of the story out?

— To win, we need a unified effort. Acts of violence by individual strikers, although understandable in terms of their frustration, might hurt us. Worse, the "strikers" might be hired infiltrators trying to provoke police action against us. How might we maintain some discipline in our ranks?

6. You might finish this part of the discussion by listing the actual subcommittees that were created:

— Relief (took care of food distribution and medical care)

— Investigation (partly to protect from provocations)

— Publicity

— Organization (among other functions, linked the subcommittees organized by ethnic groups, e.g., there were Italian relief committees and a Franco-Belgian relief committee)

— Finance (both for relief and for bail; received money as expression of labor solidarity from outside)

7. Give students **Student Handout #10-F: Lawrence Problem Solving #2.** For homework, they are to jot down ideas for each of the questions in preparation for the next day's discussion.

Procedure: Day 7

1. Reconvene the class as an IWW planning meeting, exactly as you did on Day Four. This time, the task is to develop answers to the eight questions of **Lawrence Problem Solving #2.** Remind students of their dual goal, both to win the strike and to build the union in line with IWW principles. Again, you will be present only as an observer or in order to resolve any misunderstandings of the questions on the problem-solving sheet. Students will have to organize the discussion themselves, decide how to reach a decision, and determine when an answer has been reached.

2. Again, take notes both on the class's decisions and on the decision-making process.

3. At the conclusion of the discussion, distribute the homework, **Student Handout #10-G: Lawrence, 1912—Part 3.**

Procedure: Day 8 (or so)

1. Review the eight questions of **Lawrence Problem Solving #2** one by one, asking the students to compare their own decisions with what actually happened.

2. Tell the class that a year and a half after the strike, IWW membership in Lawrence had dropped from 14,000 to 700. Ask what the reasons might have been for the decline. Make sure they remember all four factors mentioned in the homework reading: decisions made by the IWW; action by the government; the effect produced by capitalist business cycles; management strategy.

3. Ask whether the union could have acted differently to maintain its strength. (Rather than dispersing the most skilled organizers to other strikes or organizing drives, the union could have kept them in Lawrence, where they would be able to develop activities and services. The union might also have made efforts to organize all the mills in other locations owned by the same companies.)

4. Discuss with students their process of decision-making:

— Did the process of problem-solving improve from the first time to the second?

— The IWW placed great importance on workers making decisions themselves, without union officials telling them what to do. Based on your experience together, do you see any reasons the IWW would think this process so important?

— As a class, what difficulties did you have in making decisions that a group of workers might also encounter?

— What kind of decision-making skills are taught as part of your education? Are you encouraged to work and think together without an authority figure leading you?

— If not, why isn't this skill taught more widely?

— Would any groups in society feel threatened if high schools graduated students who were comfortable making decisions collectively and who expected to continue to operate that way in their work lives?

Procedure: Day 9 (optional)

This part of the lesson is optional since the concepts it presents, although extremely important, are difficult. It would require a relatively skilled class.

1. Remind the class of the earlier discussion about IWW goals: the IWW aimed not only to win strikes and build a union but to develop a society in which there are no longer owners separate from the people who produce, a society in which the workers democratically control production. Recall to students your discussion about what *skills* and what *attitudes* and beliefs about themselves the IWW sought to develop (from Day 3 of the lesson). Suggest that *knowledge* might also be an aim of their organizing. Ask students:

— If the large goal is not only to win strikes but to change the overall society, what do we need to know about the obstacles? What have we learned about those obstacles from the Lawrence strike and from previous lessons?

Some sub-questions that will help suggest answers (write student contributions on the board):

— Are there groups that benefit from maintaining hierarchy and inequality? (Who in Lawrence had a stake in inequality? Who in the **Organic Goodie Simulation?** Who benefited from conflicts between skilled and unskilled in **Homestead?** etc.)

— What are the various ways that these groups can oppose workers? (Some possible answers: layoffs, moving production to places where workers aren't organized, police, passing laws, structuring the workplace to increase divisiveness.)

— How can our own attitudes and behavior hurt our chances of making larger social change? (This is a subtle, more speculative question, meant to let students take some responsibility themselves and not see only the overwhelming forces arrayed against them. Some possible answers: our own un-certainties about whether a more just, equal, and democratic society is possible; our lack of trust in our own and others' abilities; beliefs that some people are "naturally" superior or inferior; being awestruck at the power of those above us; our own mistakes in working for change.)

2. Remind students of the ways you tried to co-opt (not simply repress) their resistance in **Organic Goodie.** Point out that the union victory at Lawrence might even have co-opted or diverted the IWW goal of *larger* social change. For instance, strikers might have become complacent when they won such a significant struggle. This could happen unless workers in Lawrence came to understand that there was still much in the whole society that needed to be changed beyond what they had accomplished. Ask the class:

— What might workers in Lawrence have learned about "winning" a strike? Can "winning" mean something more than successfully securing higher wages? What changes in their own abilities or attitudes did workers "win"?

— After such a stunning victory, how would you explain to workers in Lawrence why further social change was still necessary? What social changes would need to occur to eliminate the *causes* of workers' problems: speed-ups, boring jobs, unsafe working conditions, bad housing, etc.?

3. What experiences did people in Lawrence have during the strike that allowed them to make significant changes in their lives? in their attitudes toward themselves? in their abilities to think and act effectively with others?
   Note: This question aims to explore the idea that people undergo important changes when they are involved in a struggle for something they believe in. More than this, the specific character of the strike in Lawrence enhanced people's ability to change.

UNIT IV

OUR OWN RECENT PAST

LESSON 11

IT'S A MYSTERY—WHITE WORKERS AGAINST BLACK WORKERS

In the previous unit, students examined attempts to build solidarity between workers of various backgrounds and in different positions in the workforce. The context for these efforts was escalating management control over the workplace. A major obstacle to that solidarity has been and remains racial discrimination. Racism is so deeply embedded in our society that it is often experienced by our students as part of human nature. In **It's a Mystery** we probe some of the social factors that contributed to racial hostility in the 1920s.

One focus of this lesson is to explore why unions participated in discriminatory practices. As the **Introduction** points out, unions are not only vehicles through which workers attempt to better themselves and their society, they can also embody some of the elements of the society that their members have a stake in changing.

Goals/Objectives

1. Students will understand some of the factors that contributed to racial hostility in the years immediately following World War I.

2. Students will learn that some unions, too, were not exempt from racism.

Materials Needed

- One set of clues to **Student Handout #11-A: It's a Mystery: Clues.** (Before beginning, be sure to cut these into individual clues.)

- **Student Handout #11-B: It's a Mystery: Questions** (enough for each student).

- (*Optional:* Set of clues for a mystery contained in one of Gene Stanford's books: *Developing Effective Classroom Groups* [New York: Hart Publishing Co., 1977]; or *Learning Discussion Skills Through Games* [with Barbara Dodds Stanford] [Englewood Cliffs, NJ: Prentice Hall, 1969].)

Time Required

- One class period (two if you choose the optional murder mystery), and time for students to read aloud and discuss writing assignments.

Procedure

(*Optional*: To familiarize students with solving a mystery as a group, you may want to use one of the mysteries from the Stanford books. These are fun and fairly easy for students to unravel. In our opinion, the best one is the murder mystery in *Learning Discussion Skills Through Games*, pp. 23–27.)

1. Ask students to sit in a circle.

2. Tell students that they are about to solve a mystery together. The mystery is: Why did racism against blacks in northern cities become so much more hostile and violent during and right after World War I than it had been previously?

   Explain that as a group students will try to understand this phenomenon by looking at what happened in one typical midwestern city. ("Midwest City" is based on events which took place in Dayton, Ohio. Similar conditions prevailed in many northern cities.)

3. Read or paraphrase the following for students:

Before World War I there had been racism in Midwest City—blacks did not have the jobs or social opportunities available to whites. But there was little official segregation: Blacks could eat in any restaurant, go to any movie, or live in most neighborhoods. With World War I all this changed. Suddenly the only eating places open to them were a black-owned restaurant and the railroad station. Most hotels also closed their doors to blacks. They were even barred from white-owned theaters and movie houses.

Before the war there had been no large-scale organized hostility toward blacks. But by the early 1920s, the Ku Klux Klan was one of the most powerful organizations in the city. Klan members rode up and down major streets on white horses each Saturday night. Over 10,000 people attended Klan rallies at the county fairgrounds.

So why this sudden hostility? Was it something the black residents of Midwest City had done? Something they hadn't done? Or

did it have entirely different causes? Here lies the mystery.

Each of you will be given at least one clue that will help solve the mystery. Every clue is important and can, in various ways, be used at least once. You may tell your clue to the rest of the class but you may not show it to anyone else.

As you progress, you might select someone to write the group's ideas on the blackboard or butcher paper.

---

4. Distribute **Student Handout #11-B: It's a Mystery: Questions** to each student. Review the questions on the handout to ensure that each student is clear about what is required.

   Note: The starred questions ask for opinions. Students do not need to use the clues in their answers to those questions.

5. Distribute the clues, giving one to each student.

6. Ask students to "solve" the mystery on their own. It may be valuable to review with them some of their conclusions about group decision-making techniques from the **Lawrence** lesson. As in the Lawrence role play, you should stay completely out of the discussion unless they reach a total impasse or are extremely frustrated. In this case, you might suggest that a particular student with a crucial clue speak up.

7. Afterward, use the Question Sheet as the basis for discussion. This is also an excellent opportunity to discuss class dynamics—positive and negative—in students' solution of the mystery. Both Stanford books offer valuable ideas on the "de-briefing."

   Some points to be brought out in discussion:

   — *What major changes took place in Midwest City in the period before and after World War I?*

From 1915 to 1916, as war raged in Europe, orders placed for war materiel boosted Midwest City's industrial production by two-thirds. Blacks came North searching for the jobs being opened by this production boom. Midwest City's black population grew from 1,800 in 1910 to 9,000 in 1920. The influx of new workers created a housing shortage as capital went into war production, not new homes. Competition for scarce housing was acute and prices rose accordingly. Many blacks who came to Midwest City moved into neighborhoods where poor whites, generally immigrants from Eastern Europe, had lived. Blacks were used as strikebreakers in many cities, although not in Midwest City.

— *After World War I, what problems faced Midwest City residents for which whites may have blamed blacks?*

Competition for jobs grew fierce. Unemployment—for blacks and whites—was high. After the war, as many as one-third of Midwest City's workers were without work. Some companies even fired whites in favor of hiring blacks—hoping for a more docile nonunionized workforce. Soldiers returning home found jobs and housing much harder to come by than when they had left. Many companies reduced wages in an attempt to keep profits high.

Crime grew in Midwest City after World War I. However, there was no evidence whatsoever that blacks were more heavily involved in criminal activities than were whites.

— *Are there better explanations for each problem?*

Clearly employers helped create and then played upon divisions between black and white workers. Advertising specifically for "colored workers" at a time of high white unemployment was bound to create racial antagonisms—as was firing white workers and replacing them with black workers. During the war, companies even sent trucks to the South seeking black workers. Blacks could hardly be blamed for leaving semifeudal conditions in the South when they were likely to find higher paying jobs and better working conditions in the North.

White unions were not blameless. Had they put a higher priority on building unity between workers rather than on protecting the racial purity of their crafts, some of the conflict between blacks and whites might have been reduced.

Scarcity of housing was no one individual's fault. The quest for the highest possible profits led those with capital into war industries and away from the housing industry. Likewise, the overall decline in jobs following the war was the bust side of the capitalist boom and bust cycle, and no one individual or group could really be blamed.

The increase in crime had its roots in the numerous social problems that arose immediately following the war.

— *Why were blacks singled out as scapegoats for many of these problems?*

They were easily identifiable. In addition to skin color, they differed from the long-time Midwest City residents in speech, dress, and manner. Also, employers had an interest in keeping racial tensions high and did little to discourage those who blamed the newcomers for the recent problems.

8. Ask students to think of times in their lives when they were victimized by "scapegoating" or witnessed another individual or group being blamed for something for which they weren't responsible. Have them list a number of instances. Afterward, encourage students to share examples with each other.

9. Ask students to choose one of the instances from their lists and write about it in story form. The stories should account for *why* the particular individual or group was made a scapegoat, what the real causes were for the grievance described, and how those being scapegoated responded.

10. Allow students to read their papers aloud. Encourage people to make generalizations based on the "read-around": What did they

notice about situations described in class? In what circumstances does scapegoating seem to occur? Why do people often neglect to confront the real causes for problems? What are effective methods of resistance that can be used by scapegoated individuals or groups?

11. *Option:* Should you have time, *North to Freedom?* produced by the Dayton People's History Project, is an engaging 20-minute slide-tape of the events covered in this lesson. It is available from:

Glenn Porter
1514 Nelson St.
Dayton, OH 45410
513-256-5743

Also, *The Killing Floor,* which aired on PBS in the American Playhouse series, is an exceptionally interesting account of union organizing in the Chicago stockyards and of the events surrounding the 1919 race riots in Chicago. To our knowledge the film is not in commercial distribution. Contact a local PBS affiliate to find out about its availability.

LESSON 12

SOUTHERN TENANT FARMERS' UNION: BLACK AND WHITE UNITE?

In **It's a Mystery,** students explored a number of the factors that contribute to racial antagonism. Some of those factors—such as a dramatic increase in unemployment—are not within the immediate control of workers, but others, including the whites-only policies of most unions, were controllable.

This lesson examines efforts by black and white workers to overcome deep divisions and suspicions. Students are faced with a "what would you do?" assignment that helps them understand many of the difficulties in achieving some degree of racial unity. At the same time, they realize the importance of confronting and overcoming racist attitudes. The interview with C.P. Ellis is a remarkable example of one individual's awakening to these issues.

Goals/Objectives

1. Students will explore the difficulties of farm labor organizing in the 1930s.

2. Students will understand how racism divides potential allies.

3. Students will reflect on ways to overcome racism while trying to change oppressive conditions.

Materials Needed

● **Student Handout #12-A: Southern Tenant Farmers' Union.**

● **Student Handout #12-B: Southern Tenant Farmers' Union: Oral History.**

● **Student Handout #12-C: "Why I Quit the Klan"—An Interview with C.P. Ellis.**

Time Required

● Two to three class periods.

Procedure

1. Distribute **Student Handout #12-A: Southern Tenant Farmers' Union** to students.

2. It is probably best to read the entire handout aloud to make sure students understand the background material well. After completing the reading, go back and consider the section that lists some of the attitudes the STFU organizers might have encountered.

Brainstorm about other attitudes the black and white sharecroppers might have had which could have made them resistant to organizing. Are there additional attitudes which could be built upon? Discuss briefly some of the arguments that organizers, black or white, could have used to convince members of the other race to join the union.

3. Give the writing assignment. Make sure

students understand that they are writing a dialogue where one tenant farmer is trying to convince another to join the union and that each person is of a different race. (*Option:* It may make for a more engaging assignment if students pair up and write together. In this way they could test some of their dialogues.)

4. At the completion of the assignment, ask for volunteers to read their dialogues. If time allows, you could even encourage some groups to dramatize theirs. This would allow other students to suggest alternative approaches or additional arguments.

5. Questions to raise as students share their dialogues include:

— Is it reasonable to believe that blacks and whites could unite into one union, given the history of antagonism between these groups?

— Does facing a crisis, such as the threat of losing one's land, make it more or less likely that blacks and whites could unite?

— What arguments would white plantation owners use with poorer whites to discourage them from uniting with blacks?

— What other techniques might be used to discourage joint organization?

— If you were a black farmer, what guarantees would assure you that whites in the union wouldn't be as racist as they have been outside the union?

— Would unity be more advantageous for one race than for the other, or do both have nearly equal interests in unity?

— To overcome racism, would workers have to give in to each other, or could they join together to work for their individual interests?

— What should happen, beyond making good arguments, to enable white and black farmers to work well together?

— Have you, or has anyone you know, experienced a deep change in attitude toward people of another race? If so, what happened to make this change possible?

6. **Student Handout #12-B: Southern Tenant Farmers' Union: Oral History** is available for students to read some of the first-hand experiences of organizers of that union. Students might compare their dialogues with the actual experiences of the STFU organizers.

7. **Student Handout #12-C: "Why I Quit the Klan"** is a fascinating and moving account of C.P. Ellis's transformation from a Ku Klux Klan member to a civil rights advocate and union leader. We encourage you to use this reading because it shows clearly that, given the right experiences, not just arguments, people *can* change deeply rooted attitudes.

Questions for discussion or writing:

— What conditions in C.P. Ellis's life made him receptive to the racist explanations of the KKK?

— Ellis says the first Klan meeting was "thrilling." What had been lacking in Ellis's life that made the Klan so appealing? Are there other ways to meet needs that would unite people rather than divide them?

— Whom does Ellis believe that the Klan benefited? How did those people "behind the scenes" benefit?

— While Ellis came to understand that he was being used by people in high places, other Klan members refused to believe this. Why do you think this was the case? Was Ellis simply "smarter," or could there be other reasons Klan members would resist seeing how they were being used?

— Ellis says he believes that it is possible to change the whole society, to eliminate war and conflict. Some of his friends say this is an "impossible dream." What in Ellis's life gives him such a deep confidence in the possibility for a total social change?

8. Ellis changed his attitudes in ways that, earlier, he would not have thought possible. To put students in touch with their own potential to make dramatic changes, ask class members to think of times in their lives when they changed in ways that they would never have anticipated. Ask them to list a number of instances and then have volunteers share from their lists. From these lists, students should write in story form an account of a particular change.

LESSON 13

1934 WEST COAST LONGSHORE STRIKE

It's a Mystery pointed to a major continuing obstacle to worker solidarity; this lesson focuses on a key event in the labor renewal of the 1930s. The workers' victory in the longshore strike gave a powerful impetus toward the revitalization of an existing union and toward organizing new ones. The union that eventually resulted, the International Longshoremen's and Warehousemen's Union (ILWU), is still one of the more democratic in America.

The **Homestead** lesson indicated that industrywide labor organizing would be necessary to counteract increasing concentration of ownership and growing management coordination. In **Lawrence**, students saw a successful united labor response to a number of companies, located in the same geographic area. Here students role-play an industrywide strike that took place up and down the entire West Coast. This story has most often been told from the standpoint of San Francisco, which was the hub of the strike. We've chosen to set the lesson in Portland instead. In Portland, the importance of the ties built with other groups in the region, including farmers, is particularly clear.

Goals/Objectives

1. Students will understand the role that alliances between different social groups can play in making change.

Materials Needed

● **Student Handout #13-A: Terms You Should Know.**

● **Student Handout #13-B: Portland Daily News.**

● **Student Handout #13-C: Longshoreman; Student Handout #13-D: Unemployed Person; Student Handout #13-E: Waterfront Employer; Student Handout #13-F: Farmer; Student Handout #13-G: Central Labor Council Representative.**

● **Student Handout #13-H: Questions Facing Your Group.**

● **Student Handout #13-I: Longshore Role Play: Summing Up.**

● **Background Notes: Agitate, Educate, Organize: Portland, 1934.**

● Two or three sheets of construction paper (for groups to make name placards).

Time Required

● Three to four class periods.

‖▬▬▬▬▬▬▬▬▬▬▬▬▬▬‖

Procedure: Day 1

1. Explain to the class that each student will be assigned to a group representing a real person or persons who were involved in the 1934 longshore strike.

2. Write the names of all the groups in the role play on the board.

3. Tell students that before the role play starts, it will be important for them to be familiar with certain terms. Distribute **Student Handout #13-A: Terms You Should Know,** explaining that some of these names and expressions will already be familiar from earlier lessons in the curriculum. Students should be allowed to keep these handouts as they may wish to refer to them later in the role play.

4. Distribute **Student Handout #13-B: Portland Daily News.** Read the *Portland Daily News* editorials aloud to ensure that everyone in the class understands the causes and issues in the strike. *This understanding is essential for a successful role play.*

5. Next, divide students into five groups and have them gather in different areas of the classroom. Distribute the roles (**Student Handout 13-C** through **13-G**) to the various groups. Each person in a group should, of course, receive the same role as the others in his/her group.

6. Have students read the roles to themselves. The teacher should be familiar with the content of all the roles.

7. As a way of working students into their roles, ask them to write short interior monologues describing their hopes and fears for the strike. After they've finished, students within each group should read their monologues to one another.

8. If there is time this first day, "interview" some of the people in the different groups (e.g., What do you do for a living? What kinds of problems are you having these days? How does the longshore strike affect you? Are you for or against the strike? Why? etc.) This last activity for the first day might be a good opener for the second day, depending on the time available.

Procedure: Day 2

1. Get students back in their groups.

2. Distribute **Student Handout #13-H: Questions Facing Your Group.** (If you prefer, these could simply be listed on the board.)

3. Explain to students that it has been proposed that Governor Meier of Oregon call the National Guard to Portland to protect the strikebreakers. The governor will be holding a community meeting in Portland to listen to views on the strike and on this proposal. Each social group will make a presentation at the meeting. All the presentations must include thorough answers to the questions posed in **Student Handout #13-H.** Tell students that they will meet ("caucus") with other groups to discuss positions, build alliances, and make deals, and

that this will be a good time for them to get support from other groups for the positions they favor. But first they should discuss the questions within their own groups. Tell students they should decide what they need to know from other groups in order to arrive at a definite position on the strike. Under what, if any, circumstances would they support the strike? What could they offer another group to make that group more sympathetic to their position? What pressure could one group—or one group in combination with other groups—exert on the governor to get its way? (Remind students that simply because they may not be wealthy does not mean that they lack power. Encourage them to think about the kind of leverage they have, especially if they unite with other social groups.)

Students should be given construction paper with which to make placards indicating their social group.

4. After 10 or 15 minutes of discussion, explain to students that they will now have an opportunity to "caucus" with other groups to try to agree on the different issues facing them in the strike. Tell students: "Each group will be making a speech at the community meeting on all four of the 'Questions Facing Your Group.' If Governor Meier hears the same idea from more than one group, it's possible he'll be convinced (or intimidated enough) to take the action you urge."

You may wish to suggest some types of deals and alliances that different groups can make, e.g., longshoremen to unemployed: "The six-hour day will mean more work for the unemployed. We won't give in on this demand if you won't scab on our strike." Waterfront employers to unemployed: "Come to work for us and we'll offer you secure jobs at good pay," etc.

Be sure that each group is clearly identified. At least two people from each group should stay seated so that *everyone* in the class is not roaming around. Also, tell the students who are "traveling negotiators" that they can discuss the issues only with students who remain in their seats. This will prevent all the "travelers" from huddling together and leaving out everyone else.

The amount of time given to this caucus period is flexible and depends on whether or not students are still actively engaged in discussing the issues involved in the strike.

Again, the task is for every group to arrive at answers to *all four questions* by the end of this session.

5. Let 'em loose! It will be important for you to monitor this process, pointing out unrealistic deals, helping students identify the most likely (and most unlikely) groups to consider for alliances, etc.

6. Following the caucus period, ask students to return to their groups and begin writing presentations for the community meeting.

Procedure: Day 3

1. Have students regroup.

2. Tell students to complete the writing of their presentations.

3. Students should form a large circle for the community meeting. Each group needs to be clearly identified by the appropriate name placard.

4. Appoint one student to introduce the Honorable Governor Julius L. Meier—you.

5. Governor Meier can run the meeting however he/she chooses. We would suggest that one group at a time make its presentation and submit to questioning (and arguments) by Governor Meier *and* other groups.

6. Conclude by thanking the community and explaining that, although on July 19 you put about 1,000 Oregon National Guardsmen on alert and had them stationed at Camp Wythecomb near Portland, you've decided not to call them in to protect strikebreakers.

You might point out that you were influenced by the violence in San Francisco on July 5, 1934, in which 2 longshoremen were killed and 82 people injured in clashes involving the National Guard. The resolve of the longshoremen to defend their jobs convinced you that you might have a similar confrontation in Portland should you call in the Guard. (See **Background Notes: Agitate, Educate, Organize: Portland, 1934** for details. You might also want to assign this reading to students.)

7. Distribute homework assignment, **Student Handout #13-I: Longshore Role Play: Summing Up.**

Procedure: Day 4

1. Discuss the homework. Students will be eager to find out about the actual events of the strike. Once again, see Teacher Background Notes for this. More able students could be assigned this reading for extra credit.

Teachers on the West Coast: Time permitting, you may want to locate a speaker who can describe the strike. If you teach in a city with an ILWU local (Portland, Seattle, Tacoma, Longview, Astoria, San Francisco, Oakland, Los Angeles, etc., contact the union to find out whether there is an active pensioners group in the area which would be able to provide such a speaker.

LESSON 14

III ━━━━━━━━━━ III

UNION MAIDS

The 1930s were a crucial period in shaping the labor movement that exists today. Having looked at some specific struggles, students now take an overview.

At an earlier period, in **Birth of a Rank-and-File Organizer,** we saw the development of a union activist. Here students personally meet three, and have the benefit of their hindsight in looking back at the 1930s.

The film combines the women's own lively stories with rare newsreel footage and music of the time. *Union Maids* is a "must" film for students to feel the vitality of labor organizing in the 1930s.

Goals/Objectives

1. Students will see some of the conditions that gave rise to the growth of the Congress of Industrial Organizations (CIO) in the 1930s.

2. Students will examine the reasons why some people choose to dedicate their lives to organizing other workers.

3. Students will question why labor unions were so strenuously opposed by some employers and governmental agencies in the 1930s.

Materials Needed

- Film: *Union Maids*. This is available from:

    New Day Films
    P.O. Box 315
    Franklin Lakes, NJ 07417

    Many colleges, libraries, women's centers, and labor unions also own and loan out copies of the film. We would urge you to request your local school district audio visual department to obtain a copy.

- **Student Handout #14: Union Maids: Letter from a Relative.**

Time Required

- Two class periods with homework (the film is 48 minutes long).

III ━━━━━━━━━━ III

Procedure

1. Before the film, review the following terminology: AFL craft unionism, industrial unionism, scab, yellow dog contract, picket line, picket captain, blacklist, solidarity.

2. Immediately preceeding the film, ask students to take out a sheet of paper and make two columns. The first column should be headed *Conditions Needing Change;* the other column, *Methods Used.* Tell students that as they watch the film they should list in the first column all the things the women didn't like about their work and their conditions of life. In the second column they should in-

clude all the methods the women used to try to change those conditions.

3. Show the film.

4. Have students use their lists as a basis for discussing these questions:

— What were some of the things the women didn't like and wanted to change about their jobs? How about things in their lives away from the job?

— All of the women in the film saw themselves as "organizers"—people who try to make changes. From the stories they told, what do organizers do? What does it mean to be an organizer? Think, for example, of the kinds of actions Sylvia took in her workplace to achieve change.

— Why did the women become organizers?

— Did they have any important "role models"?

— Do you think that any of the women saw their organizer role as a "sacrifice"? Were these women just working for other people, or were they also working for themselves? (*Note:* In the **Organic Goodie** lesson, **Student Handout #1-B: Can People Act Together?,** students were asked to write about a time when they had worked or acted for other people while they worked for themselves as well. If you did not assign the writing earlier, now might be a good time.)

— Do you think that being workers and also organizers made their jobs more interesting? More fun? In what ways?

— What were some of the risks the women took? What additional risks might organizers face?

— In what ways did companies try to resist the union organizing of that time? In what ways did the companies try to divide workers? What attempts did the three women make to overcome those divisions?

— How does Sylvia say her ideas about white people changed? Are there similarities between how Sylvia's ideas about white people changed and the changes in C.P. Ellis's views of black people?

— In **Birth of a Rank-and-File Organizer,** we discussed whether union recognition would mean everyone would live "happily ever after." Do Stella, Kate, and Sylvia think that, having won many of the battles of the 1930s, things are wonderful now? What do they feel unions should be doing today?

5. After this discussion, distribute **Student Handout #14: Union Maids: Letter from a Relative.** Encourage students to use a number of examples, even tapping their own imaginations, in completing the letter. When students have finished the assignment, ask for volunteers to read their letters. Discuss Kate's life and the satisfactions she derived from her experiences as an organizer as well as what she contributed to the society as a whole.

UNIT V

CONTINUING STRUGGLE

LESSON 15

SHUTDOWN!
CONFRONTING PLANT CLOSURES

The era of union growth, followed by stability, that began in the 1930s is ending. Despite today's decline in union membership, however, there are indications of new issues and new coalitions arising. Out of them will come the labor movement of the next period in U.S. history.

In this lesson, students grapple with one of the difficult and unresolved issues of the present: plant closures. For some, they will be drawing on their own experiences or the recent past of their own community. Depending on the choices students make, they will be using much of what they may have learned in previous lessons about cooperating among themselves, restructuring work, and seeking potential allies outside the labor movement.

Goals/Objectives

1. Students will understand some of the personal and community consequences of closing facilities that provide employment.

2. Students will enhance their ability to think about public policy and evaluate appropriate means and ends.

3. Students will learn some of the limits to any choice that unions and workers in a particular facility may make in response to a closure.

Materials Needed

- A large sheet of butcher paper.

- **Student Handout #15-A: Plant Closures Fact Sheet.**

- **Student Handout #15-B: First Responses.**

- **Student Handouts #15-C through 15-F: Option Sheets.**

- **Student Handout #15-G: The Action Is Today!**

Time Required

- Three and one-half class periods.

Procedure: Day 1

1. Pick a large employer in the community, one that students are likely to know about through their own or their parents' jobs, and ask students to imagine the consequences were it to shut completely and permanent-ly. The example could be a store, hotel, government bureau, or office, as well as a factory. Where the community has experienced a recent real-life instance of a major shutdown, draw on it.

2. Ask students how they themselves might be affected. Some questions include:

— Have any of you experienced layoffs yourselves or among your families or friends?

— What would it feel like to be laid off? What if you were a major wage-earner in the family?

— What might be some consequences for life in the family?

— What would be some of the effects on the whole community of a large number of people losing their jobs?

— Are places where students typically work likely to be affected by a shutdown elsewhere in town—if, for instance, there is less money available for shopping or eating out?

— How would school or community programs be affected?

3. Post a sheet of butcher paper. Using the same example of a hypothetical or recent shutdown in your community, have the students brainstorm a network of the shutdown's consequences. Write the conse-

quences on the butcher paper, drawing lines to indicate which factors interconnect with which others. The network of these interconnections forms a *Cluster Chart.* (For example, if students point to increased tensions at home—say depression or spouse abuse—you might ask what additional consequences follow. The need for more social services, then, would intersect with fewer public resources available because of the lower tax base due to the shutdown. See the sample *Cluster Chart.*) Save the *Cluster Chart* for later use.

4. When the brainstorming has slowed down, distribute **Student Handout #15-A: Plant Closures Fact Sheet.** Encourage students to use this to suggest any additions to the *Cluster Chart.* In particular, ask what groups in the community might be affected by the shutdown.

5. Explain to students that they are to imagine themselves as workers in a factory that is about to close, and that they will work together in small groups to plan their response. Distribute **Student Handout #15-**

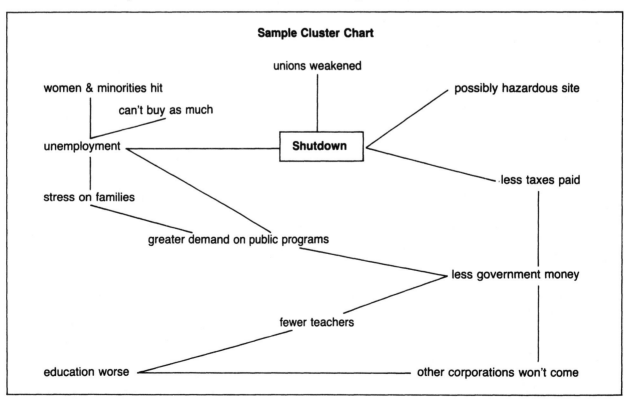

Sample Cluster Chart

B: First Responses. For the remainder of the period, they should read over this description of the community and how workers first responded to news of the imminent shutdown. If there is time, they may begin the homework that accompanies the reading.

Procedure: Day 2

1. Remind students they are workers in the factory that is going to close. You are the elected president of their local union and you call the union meeting to order. Play this role as a good union officer would: responsive to the membership, encouraging democratic processes.

2. Tell students that this special meeting has been called to figure out the union's response to the shutdown announcement. The meeting will form subcommittees to investigate various alternatives. There will be information on how other workers in comparable situations have acted.

3. Put up the *Cluster Chart* from Day One. Before weighing the alternative strategies, the meeting might want to consider whether there are any allies who might join in actions to oppose shutdowns. To think of possible allies, members may draw on the *Cluster Chart,* as well as on their knowledge of the community. (Since the discussion at this stage is speculative, students may fill in the gaps in their knowledge of the community by drawing on what they know about their own community and by using their imaginations.) Ask the following:

— Other than the workers, who else might be affected by a shutdown?

— Would workers or their families be members of community groups that might have a stake in opposing the shutdown?

— What are the ways we could gain support from the groups we've identified?

4. List the following alternatives on the board:

— Plant closure legislation.

— Government relief for the company.

— Take over the plant and run it ourselves.

— Persuade or force the company to stay.

5. Inform the meeting that these alternatives, or some mix of them, have been workers' responses in situations similar to our own. The union will form committees to investigate each of these alternatives and report back to the meeting for a discussion and vote. Give brief summaries of each option, drawing on the introductory paragraphs of the option sheets. You might also want to point out some of the general differences among the options: i.e., which accept or reject in principle the right of the company to close, which permit the workers to keep more initiative in their own hands, and which leave initiative more with the company or government.

6. Divide the meeting into four committees, distributing the appropriate **Student Handouts #15-C, 15-D, 15-E,** and **15-F: Option Sheets** to each member (each committee is to receive only the option sheets for the alternative it is investigating). If the committees are too large for full participation in discussing the questions, they should be divided in half.

7. Tell students that each committee must respond to every question on its handout and that it will be questioned by the other groups. Each group may decide the best way to make its presentation. Remind the committees that they need not favor their assigned alternative, only investigate it. Tell them, in fact, that it is likely that some of the groups will end up opposing the choices they are exploring. Give them a few minutes to read the sheets before the committee discussions begin. (*Note:* Committees may

or may not choose to have chairpeople to facilitate their discussions.)

8. If the committees have not finished their work by the end of class, encourage students to continue individually overnight. Committees also may choose to apportion overnight responsibility for specific questions to individual members.

Procedure: Day 3

1. Once the committees have finished their work, tell students it is time for the groups to report to the larger union meeting, following which the entire meeting will vote on a course of action.

2. Ask one of the groups to give a summary of its investigation and conclusions, then open the meeting to questions and reactions. Encourage questions that are not only informational but that may challenge the committee's conclusions. Continue until each of the groups has reported and been questioned.

3. Announce that the meeting is now open for motions on adopting particular alternatives or combinations of alternatives. With each motion, permit discussion pro and con. As president, you may certainly question whether the union has sufficient resources for the alternatives proposed.

4. Once the meeting has voted for a particular course of action, it is time to consider possible community support in greater depth. The specific discussion will depend on how much the issue was dealt with during the discussion of alternatives. Make sure, however, that the following questions are answered:

— In light of what we've decided about how to oppose the shutdown, what community groups might we approach as possible coalition partners?

— What could we as workers offer these groups that would be in their interest and in ours to get them to join a coalition? Make this discussion as concrete as possible, i.e., what specific support would be possible on what issues of concern to each of the potential partners?

5. Adjourn the meeting and distribute homework: **Student Handout #15-G: The Action Is Today!** If time permits, you might want to read or have a student read aloud the main speech in that assignment.

Procedure: Day 4

1. Debrief the students about their participation in the role play and their conclusions. The appropriate questions will depend in part on what was and was not covered in the discussion during the union meeting. You might ask:

— Were the conclusions of each committee questioned effectively by other groups? Were there grounds for question or challenge that weren't raised?

— Was there a clearcut choice among the alternatives, one that had no or few limits or disadvantages?

— If the course of action chosen were to be successful, would it prevent shutdowns in the future in this workplace? Would it prevent shutdowns affecting workers everywhere in the country?

— In your opinion: What are the limits on what could be accomplished by only one union? By unions acting together but without support from other community groups? How big a change in the whole society would be necessary to solve the problem of plant closures?

2. Depending on the choices students made, both among the possible responses to the shutdown and in how they worked together, this can be a good occasion to remind them of past lessons. Some possible questions:

— When we did the **Organic Goodie Simulation,** one of the issues was whether or not we thought people were able to get together, based on their common interests, to change a bad or oppressive situation. Do your conclusions in **Shutdown!** show that you've changed your minds about that possibility? Why or why not?

— In both the **West Coast Longshore Strike** role play and earlier in **Lawrence, 1912,** enlisting the support of the community was crucial to the outcome. Could we have done more of that to oppose the factory closure? Why didn't we do more of that? What more could have been accomplished with community support?

LESSON 16

III ———————————————— III

LABOR SONGS

Culture, and music in particular, can play a large role in sustaining a common sense of interests, goals, and expectations. When labor culture has declined, so has people's ability to work together. Labor songs are therefore much more than simply work songs. They help create solidarity and understanding.

Lawrence, 1912, was known as the "singing strike." Students may have already heard the song "Bread and Roses" and discussed the role of singing in that strike. Here they're not only introduced to some further labor classics, but they're given the opportunity to reflect on what they've learned of labor history by creating their own songs and poems.

Goals/Objectives

1. Students will analyze and evaluate songs that have played a role in U.S. labor history.

2. Students will summarize their understanding of, and appreciation for, labor history through poem and song.

Materials Needed

● Several photographs of work or strike scenes.

● **Student Handout #16: Labor Songs.**

Time Required

● Two or three class periods—flexible.

III ———————————————— III

Procedure: Day 1

1. Play or read the songs included on **Student Handout #16: Labor Songs.**

2. The following are some discussion questions based on the songs:

Solidarity Forever

— According to the song, what are unions for?

— What injustices are unions supposed to help people overcome?

— Who is the "we" in "It's we who plowed the prairies . . ."

— What can "the power in our hands" be used for according to the song?

— What do you think the song writer wants the "new world" to be like?

Union Maid

— What makes this union maid so fearless?

— What gave courage to Kate, Sylvia, and Stella—the women in the film *Union Maids*?

— The song anticipates that union organizing will be met by resistance. According to the song, who will oppose efforts to organize?

— Is this borne out in our study of workers' attempts to organize?

— Do you think women might have problems today in trying to "organize the guys"?

— The third verse suggests that perhaps women will have problems even in the union. What might some of these problems be?

— Is the song optimistic about overcoming those problems? If so, do you agree?

— According to the song, how has the role of women changed in the United States?

— The fourth verse states that women want more than just higher pay. What other goals do you think are important and worth fighting for?

— What role could a union play in working on these other issues?

Casey Jones

— Why do you think Casey might have refused to join the strike?

— In the strikes we've studied, how have "scabs" been treated by strikers?

— Is the song consistent or inconsistent with that treatment?

— What is the "moral" of the song?

— Do you agree with that moral? Why or why not?

Hallelujah I'm a Bum

— Why doesn't the character in the song go to work?

— Whom does he blame for being out of work?

— Why do you think the questioner in the first line does not understand the problems of the other person?

— How does the unemployed person survive?

— What might have been going on in the United States when this song was written?

— In the last verse, why will the boss be broke if he pays out all the money his workers earn?

— According to the song, what do bosses do?

The Ballad of Joe Hill

(*Note:* Joe Hill was arrested in Utah and accused of murdering a grocer and his son. Many people claimed that Hill was framed because he was an IWW member and gave encouragement to organizing drives through his songs. His impending execution was protested by hundreds of thousands of people throughout the world. Joe Hill was executed on November 19, 1915. The last words he spoke were, "Don't mourn for me—organize!")

— What does Joe Hill mean by saying "I never died"?

— In what ways did Joe Hill go on living?

— What did "they" forget to kill?

— Could they have killed that?

Procedure: Day 2

1. Choose several pictures—contemporary and historical—that portray work or strike scenes of some kind. Try to select ones that you feel might spark some creativity in students. Be sure to choose pictures which also include women, as many labor photo anthologies focus almost exclusively on men.

2. Ask students to take out a sheet of paper.

3. As you show each photo to the entire class, have students brainstorm on paper the words and phrases that come to mind.

4. After you have shown all the photographs, tell students that you want them to write a poem or song using some of the words on their lists. Encourage students to relate these writings to the history and concepts they've explored in recent lessons. You might also review with students some of the themes in the songs they listened to earlier.

Students might:

(1) Choose to write about a particular incident—e.g., the 1934 longshore strike, tenant farmer organizing, etc.

(2) Relate present labor/working problems or problems they have experienced personally to those of the past.

(3) Choose an issue the labor movement *should* be addressing.

(4) Summarize their overall feelings/observations about working people's experiences/labor processes/organization, etc.

Those unfamiliar with writing poetry may need your help. Obviously, students needn't use words from their lists if these don't inspire them. But we've found that students feel they've already begun their poems if they've put at least some words down on paper.

5. Allow the rest of the period to get started. Students should finish their poems or songs as homework.

6. Ask for student volunteers to read their poems or sing their songs. Discuss with the class the relationship of the writing to the issues raised throughout their study of the history of work and workers.

STUDENT HANDBOOK

STUDENT HANDOUT #1-A

ORGANIC GOODIE SIMULATION
Questions

1. What were the various ways that I tried to create divisions between people in the role play?

2. What actions did you personally take to try and stop my efforts to divide people?

3. If we were to do this simulation again, what different actions would you take?

4. Comment on the cartoon on the left, published by the United Electrical, Radio and Machine Workers of America. Does it relate to our role play? If so, how?

STUDENT HANDOUT #1-B

CAN PEOPLE ACT TOGETHER?

1. Can people really stick together, look out for each other and work together for common goals—or are people mostly out for themselves? Explain your answer.

2. Is it possible to be out for yourself and still act together with others? Explain.

3. Think of a specific time in your life when you have been able to act together with other people. Describe the circumstances and what you think made it possible for people to stick together.

4. Why do people have a hard time working together for common goals? Is it because of human nature (that's the way people are—all people)? Is it because of what people are taught or the pressures they're under? Are there other reasons?

STUDENT HANDOUT #2

A WORKER READS HISTORY
by Bertolt Brecht

Who built the seven towers of Thebes?
The books are filled with names of kings.
Was it kings who hauled the craggy blocks of stone?
And Babylon, so many times destroyed,
Who built the city up each time? In which of Lima's houses,
That city glittering with gold, lived those who built it?
In the evening when the Chinese wall was finished
Where did the masons go? Imperial Rome
Is full of arcs of triumph. Who reared them up? Over whom
Did the Caesars triumph? Byzantium lives in song,
Were all her dwellings palaces? And even in Atlantis of the legend
The night the sea rushed in,
The drowning men still bellowed for their slaves.

Young Alexander plundered India.
He alone?
Caesar beat the Gauls.
Was there not even a cook in his army?
Philip of Spain wept as his fleet
Was sunk and destroyed. Were there no other tears?
Frederick the Great triumphed in the Seven Years War. Who
Triumphed with him?

Each page a victory,
At whose expense the victory ball?
Every ten years a great man,
Who paid the piper?

So many particulars.
So many questions.

From *Selected Poems,* copyright 1947 by Bertolt Brecht and H.R. Hays. Reprinted by permission of Harcourt Brace Jovanovich, Inc.

STUDENT HANDOUT #3-A

LABOR MOVEMENT
What We Do and Don't Yet Know

1. How long have there been unions or similar forms of worker organization?

   (a) Since the different craftspeople built Noah's ark
   (b) Since the time of the great Egyptian pyramids
   (c) Since the brewers and weavers in the Middle Ages
   (d) Since railroads were built in the nineteenth century
   (e) Since the sit-down strikes of the 1930s

2. What do unions do? List all the important things you can think of.

3. Most public school teachers in the United States are represented by a union: true or false?

4. Imagine a large and complex workplace, say a factory that builds trucks. There are people doing many kinds of jobs: operators of metal-cutting machines, electricians, painters, workers to assemble the trucks, maintenance workers, office workers, etc. If this were a union workplace, how many unions would you be likely to find?

5. Which of the following were created as a result of workers' struggles or organizing?
   (a) Social Security
   (b) Workers' compensation (for people injured on the job)
   (c) Unemployment benefits
   (d) Minimum wage
   (e) Cure for the common cold
   (f) Child labor laws (protecting children from heavy work and long hours)
   (g) Public education
   (h) The Cincinnati Redstockings (the first professional baseball team)

STUDENT HANDOUT #3-B

WHAT RIGHTS DO I HAVE?
(Part 1)

In the following drama, *you* are the main character. Use your imagination to think how you might respond. Give your best guess about what rights you have. Remember, rights are changeable. Your rights were won because people worked for them. Rights you don't have could still be won. Your rights as a citizen might or might not apply in the workplace.

You work in a large office. Your pay is not high, and you don't have much money saved. You've always been something of a fighter, standing up for your rights and encouraging your friends to do the same. You've just been transfered to another part of the office under a different supervisor.

1. Your supervisor asks you to spend the week working with some chemicals for the office copiers. You've heard of other people getting sick by handling office machine chemicals and are reluctant to do it yourself unless you know that the chemicals are safe. Your supervisor gives you a direct order to do the job. "What is this, the army?" you say.

   (a) Do you have a right to know what chemicals you're handling and if they're safe?

   (b) Do you have a right to refuse work that you're pretty sure is seriously dangerous to your health?

   (c) What will you do?

2. You've investigated and found that coming in contact with some office machine chemicals for more than a limited time can indeed be hazardous to your health and to the health of any children you might want to have. That could be true either by breathing the fumes or through direct skin contact. As a result, you refuse to obey your supervisor. The supervisor charges you with insubordination and suspends you from work.

(a) Do you have a right to a hearing at which you can defend yourself?

(b) Do you have the right to be represented by someone at a hearing?

3. You print a leaflet about the unsafe working conditions. When you post one on the bulletin board, the supervisor tears it down. When you try to hand out the leaflet in your office, the supervisor confiscates all your copies. "I thought this was a free country!" you say.

(a) Do you have a right to do what you did? What *are* your rights of free speech in the workplace?

(b) Should you have a right to do what you did with the leaflets?

4. You go to a meeting of the union for your office and ask the union to call a strike because of your suspension and because of unsafe working conditions.

(a) Does the union have a right to strike for these reasons?

(b) Should it have that right?

STUDENT HANDOUT #3-C

WHAT RIGHTS DO I HAVE?
(Part 2)

1. What rights do people have as citizens that may not apply in the workplace?

2. Should your constitutional rights to free speech, a fair trial, etc., apply in the workplace? Give reasons for your answer.

3. Compare what you know about rights in the workplace with rights you have in school. Give some specific examples.

STUDENT HANDOUT #4

FREDERICK WINSLOW TAYLOR
Taylorisms

Taylor's Process:

Before: "The shop [factory] was really run by the workmen and not by the bosses. The workmen together had carefully planned just how fast each job should be done. The manager fully realizes that the combined knowledge and skill of the workmen who were under him was certainly ten times as great as his own."

Stage One: "Managers assume the burden of gathering together all of the traditional knowledge which in the past has been possessed by the workmen and then classifying, tabulating, and reducing this knowledge to rules, laws, formulae."

Stage Two: "All possible brainwork should be removed from the shop and centered in the planning or laying out department."

Stage Three: "The work of every workman is fully planned out by the management at least one day in advance, and each man receives in most cases complete written instructions, describing in detail the task which he is to accomplish, as well as the means to be used in doing the work: not only what is to be done, but *how* it is to be done and the exact time allowed for doing it."

Effect: "The full possibilities of my system will not have been realized until almost all of the machines in the shop are run by men who are of smaller calibre and attainments and who are therefore cheaper than those required under the old system."

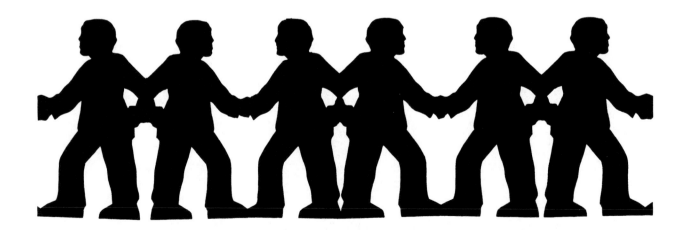

STUDENT HANDOUT #5

FREE TO THINK, TALK, LISTEN, OR SING

As industry became bigger and more mechanized, thousands of skilled craftsmen saw the nature of their work change. In 1883, a young mechanic described to a United States Senate committee the shifts taking place in his trade:

The trade has been subdivided and those subdivisions have been again subdivided, so that a man never learns the machinist's trade now. Ten years ago he learned, not the whole trade, but a fair portion of it. Also, there is more machinery used in the business, which again makes machinery. . . . It is merely laborers' work. . . .

One man may make just a particular part of a machine and may not know anything whatever about another part of the same machine. In that way machinery is produced a great deal cheaper than it used to be formerly, and in fact, through this system of work, 100 men are able to do now what it took 300 or 400 men to do fifteen years ago. . . . They so simplify the work that it is made a great deal easier and put together a great deal faster. There is no system of apprenticeship, I may say, in the business. You simply go in and learn whatever branch you are put at, and you stay at that unless you are changed to another. . . .

Did such specialized work have any effect on a man's thinking?

It has a very demoralizing effect upon the mind throughout. The man thinks of nothing else but that particular branch; he knows that he cannot leave that particular branch and go to any other; he has got no chance whatever to learn anything else because he is kept steadily and constantly at that particular thing.

Could a man working in a machine shop hope to rise, to become a boss or a manufacturer himself?

There is no chance. They have lost all desire to become bosses now . . . because the trade has become demoralized. First they earn so small wages; and, next, it takes so much capital to become a boss now that they cannot think of it, because it takes all they can earn to live.

One immigrant from England wrote back to his friends in Sheffield:

They do far more with machinery in all trades than you do. Men never learn to do a knife through, as they do in Sheffield. The knives go through forty or fifty hands.

Shoemakers, tailors, dyers, tanners arriving hopefully from abroad, found work in the United States quite unlike what they knew back home. It was chiefly workers in the building trades who found their craft was not being replaced by machinery. The machine was slow to enter mining and railway construction, too. But in iron, steel, and textiles change was very rapid.

The skilled puddler and boiler saw their jobs disappear when Bessemer and open-hearth furnaces took over production of steel ingots. The output of Bessemer ingots jumped nine times between 1874 and 1882. In the cotton and wool industries, too, a new technique called ring-spinning replaced mule-spinning, a highly skilled occupation. One mill superintendent told a reporter this story:

The mule-spinners are a tough crowd to deal with. A few years ago they were giving trouble at this mill, so one Saturday afternoon, after they had gone home, we started right in and smashed up a room-full of mules with sledgehammers. When the men came back on Monday morning, they were astonished to find that there was no work for them. That room is now full of ring frames run by girls.

The shoe industry was the classic example of what was happening. Pressed by Civil War demands for huge quantities of shoes, the mill owners introduced automatic machinery. Asked by a Congressional committee in 1899 to describe changes in work and wages in his trade, a leader of the Boot and Shoe Workers' Union said:

Eleven years ago I used to be able to earn myself, lasting shoes, from $18 to $35 in a week, according to how hard I wanted to work; that is, in the city of Lynn. Today, on the same class of work, I would not be able, on any job in the city, to make over $15, and probably my wage would run nearer $12. . . . And another thing: where a man at that time would likely get eight or nine months' good work in a year, at the present time the season is shorter. . . . The manufacturers equip themselves to turn out their product in a shorter time, and the seasons of employment are shorter and more uncertain.

With about one hundred subdivisions of labor in the making of a shoe, the worker became specialized in one simple operation. Asked what effect that had upon him, Mr. Eaton replied:

He becomes a mere machine. . . . Take the proposition of a man operating a machine to nail on 40 to 60 cases of heels in a day. That is 2,400 pairs, 4,800 shoes, in a day. One not accustomed to it would wonder how a man could pick up and lay down 4,800 shoes in a day, to say nothing of putting them on a jack into a machine and having them nailed on. That is the driving method of the manufacture of shoes under these minute subdivisions.

The effect was to multiply production. By 1885 the Massachusetts factories were making four times as many cases of boots and shoes as they had made two decades earlier. The art of shoemaking, as an individual craft, became a thing of the past. The old-time shoe shop, a small room perhaps ten by fourteen, disappeared. Remembering how different the workman's life was then, Mr. Eaton said:

In these old shops, years ago, one man owned the shop; he took in work and three, four, five, or six others, neighbors, came in there and sat down and made shoes right in their laps, and there was no machinery. Everybody was at liberty to talk; they were all politicians. . . . Of course, under these conditions, there was absolute freedom and exchange of ideas, they naturally would become more intelligent than shoe workers can at the present time, when they are driving each man to see how many shoes he can handle, and where he is surrounded by noisy machinery. And another thing, this nervous strain on a man doing just one thing over and over again must necessarily have a wearing effect on him; and his ideals, I believe, must be lowered.

The shoemakers looked back regretfully on their recent past. It had been the usual practice in those days for cobblers to hire a boy to read aloud from books on philosophy or history or science. It was nothing to interrupt a task in order to debate a fine point in the text. But now "the gentle craft of leather" was gone, and the artisan had become nothing more than "a tender to the machine."

Something of the same nostalgia was voiced by the cigarmaker Samuel Gompers in his autobiography:

The craftsmanship of the cigarmaker was shown in his ability to utilize wrappers to the best advantage, to shave off the unusable to a hairbreadth, to roll so as to cover holes in the leaf and to use both hands so as to make a perfectly shaped and rolled product. These things a good cigarmaker learned to do more or less mechanically, which left us free to think, talk, listen, or sing. I loved the freedom of that work, for I had earned the mind-freedom that accompanied skill as a craftsman. I was eager to learn from discussion and reading or to pour out my feeling in song. Often we chose someone to read to us who was a particularly good reader, and in payment the rest of us gave him sufficient of our cigars so he was not the loser. The reading was always followed by discussion, so we learned to know each other pretty thoroughly. We learned who could take a joke in good spirit, who could marshal his thoughts in an orderly way, who could distinguish clever sophistry from sound reasoning. The fellowship that grew between congenial shopmates was something that lasted a lifetime.

As the brick walls of the factories closed in on them, the workers' sense of personal freedom slipped away. One Massachusetts mechanic in 1879 described the atmosphere in a shop employing 100 to 125 men:

During working hours the men are not allowed to speak to each other, though working close together, on pain of instant discharge. Men are hired to watch and patrol the shop. The workers of Massachusetts have always been law and order men. We loved our country, and respected the laws. For the last five years the times have been growing worse every year, until we have been brought down so far that we have not much further to go. What do the mechanics of Massachusetts say to each other? I will tell you: "We must have a change. Any thing is better than this. We cannot be worse off, no matter what the change is."

The same worker also said:

I work harder now than when my pay was twice as large. Less than five years ago wages were from $12 to $18 a week currency; now they are from $6 to $12, and work not as steady.

Ten years later, in 1889, the payroll for the Lyman cotton mill in Holyoke, Massachusetts, showed wages in the cording room running as low as $.05 an hour. Here are some samples taken from its ledger:

Job	Total hours	Price per hour	Weekly amount
Section hand	60	$ .20	$12.00
Third oiler	60	.10	6.00
Scrubber	60	.05	3.00
Picker man	60	.10	6.00
Stripper	60	.09½	5.70
Lap oiler	60	.08½	5.10
Grinder	60	.15	9.00
Railways & drawing	60	.07	4.20

There was a common saying in those days, heard often from housewives: "You go to market with the money in a basket, and carry home the goods in your pocket." To see what a millhand's wages could buy, let's look at these figures on the weekly cost of living taken from a New York labor paper, *The Printer*, of August 1864. These are the actual expenses for a family of six—father, mother, and four children:

Expenditures for the Week

1 bag of flower	$1.80
small measure of potatoes daily at $.17 per day for 7 days	1.19
¼ pound of tea	.38
1 pound coffee (mixed or adulterated, can't afford better)	.35
3½ pounds sugar	1.05
milk	.56
meats for the week (being on ½ ration supply)	3.50
2 bushels of coal	1.36
4 pounds butter	1.60
2 pounds lard	.38
kerosene	.30
soap, starch, pepper, salt, vinegar, etc.	1.00
vegetables	.50
dried apples (to promote health of children)	.25
sundries	.28
rent	4.00
	$18.50

The Printer noted the average wage for all branches of the trade locally was $16 a week. (Workers in other trades got as little as $3, $4, or $6 a week.) This family, then, spent $2.50 more than the father earned, and had nothing left for clothing or entertainment. The paper added, "The fortunate printer that has more than one suit to his back, or whose wife can boast of more than a change of calicoes, can scarcely be found."

Hours of work were as long as wages were short. The men driving the horse-drawn streetcars of New York City in the 1880s worked fourteen to sixteen hours a day in all weather. Their pay was $1.75 a day. What it was like to work a fourteen-hour day is told by Ira Steward, a machinist who devoted his life to the cause of a shorter work week. He wrote in *Fincher's Trades' Review*, October 14, 1865:

Take the average operative or mechanic employed by a corporation fourteen hours a day. His labor commences at half-past four in the morning, and does not cease until half-past seven p.m. How many newspapers or books can he read? What time has he to visit or receive visits? to take baths? to write letters? to cultivate flowers? to walk with his family? Will he not be quite as likely to vote in opposition to his real interests as in favor? What is his opinion good for? Will anyone ask his advice? What will he most enjoy, works of art or rum? Will he go to meeting on Sunday? Does society care whether he is happy or miserable? sick or well? dead or alive? How often are his eyes tempted by the works of art? His home means to him his food and his bed. His life is work, with the apparition, however, of some time being without, for his work means bread! "Only that and nothing more." He is debased by excessive toil! He is almost without hope!

Think how monotonous that path leading from house to factory, and from factory to house again—the same sidewalk every day, rain or shine, summer or winter—leading by the same low houses—inhabited by beings walking the same social treadmill as himself. Half-past seven comes at last, and as the wheel stops he catches his coat, and half staggering with fatigue, hurries homeward in the darkness, thinking of nothing but food and rest.

This reading is taken from Milton Meltzer, *Bread and Roses: The Struggle of American Labor, 1865–1915,* copyright © 1967 by Milton Meltzer. Reprinted by permission of Alfred A. Knopf, Inc.

Assignment:
Imaginative Writing

1. Imagine you are a worker who has just gotten a job in a factory that has introduced new machinery and assembly-line techniques. Before this new job, you worked as a skilled craftsman in conditions similar to those described by Samuel Gompers or Mr. Eaton of the Boot and Shoe Workers' Union. Write a letter back to your former workmates telling them about your new job. In the letter explain your new conditions of work, how these compare to your earlier conditions, how this affects relations between workers, how your personal and family life have changed, and how all this makes you feel. Be specific, be imaginative.

or

2. The industrial changes described in the reading gave rise to unions formed by workers. Pretend you are a worker in a Massachusetts shoe factory who has been assigned to draw up a leaflet or pamphlet detailing the demands of your union. Be specific, be eloquent and, if you like, be artistic.

STUDENT HANDOUT #7-A

"TAYLORIZING" BURGERS
A Fantasy

It wasn't often that Frederick Winslow Taylor IV felt like eating hamburgers. Generally, he was fond of steak. But as it happened that evening, he found himself walking into the All-American Deluxe Hamburger Shoppe.

Choosing a seat by the window, Taylor sat down, picked up a menu, and began wondering whether he'd have a cheeseburger, a double hamburger, or a bacon and sprouts burger.

"Well, forget you! I don't care if you are chef, waiter, and cashier all rolled into one! I'm the owner here and what I say goes! Got that, pal? What I say goes!"

The man stormed out of the kitchen into the restaurant. When he discovered that all customers' eyes were upon him, he promptly turned a deep red. Still shaking, he stood fumbling with his tie and tried to recapture his lost dignity.

With the excitement over, the two dozen or so customers resumed chomping on their All-American Deluxe Burgers or slurping their All-American Deluxe Milkshakes or munching their All-American Deluxe French Fries.

But Taylor's curiosity was aroused. Of course, he was no *ordinary* customer. And as the still-red owner was trying to make his way out, Frederick caught hold of his arm.

"Problems with your workers, I see."

The owner grunted.

"You know," Taylor continued, "I just might be able to help you out. Ever heard of Frederick W. Taylor?"

"Who?"

"My great-great-grandfather—Frederick W. Taylor. You *have* heard of him, haven't you? He was *the* expert in dealing with workers, a true scientist of the work process, a master of management." He beamed with pride.

"So?" snapped the owner.

"So, I too know a great deal about the problems we owners and managers face, and I'm offering you my scientific assistance. Please join me, won't you?"

The owner, having regained his composure, was just curious (and desperate) enough to agree. And sitting down asked, "Okay, Taylor, how can *you* help *me?*"

Well, first I need to know what's the problem. Any owner who has to remind his workers who's boss definitely has a problem," he chuckled.

The owner, not amused, thought for a moment. "I guess I've just let the workers take advantage of me. You see, I used to believe that if my workers helped run the restaurant, they'd feel like it was *theirs* and things would go more smoothly."

"Aha!" Taylor smiled knowingly. "As I suspected. You let the workers control the restaurant, and they fouled things up and now you're going broke. Right?"

"Wrong," the owner shook his head. "No, the restaurant is making a profit."

"It is?" Taylor looked puzzled. "So what's your problem?"

"The problem is that the workers want to decide everything themselves. They want to change the menu. They insist on offering what they claim are more nutritional foods. Well, that's fine. But you know these health foods take more time to prepare, and my profits aren't as high as they *could* be. I might even have to hire more workers! They also set their own schedules and sometimes don't come in if they're just barely not feeling well or even if they're tired of working! I don't have to pay them if they don't come in, of course, but it makes planning more difficult for me."

Taylor nodded his head, "Well this *is* troubling, though my great-great-grandfather faced much stickier problems."

The owner ignored him. "I never should have started this decision-sharing. It's just gotten totally out of hand. Imagine: all my workers are chefs, they all wait on tables, they all make up the recipes and order food, they're all cashiers. They're all everything."

Frederick W. Taylor IV scratched his head and frowned. "How can all your employees be chefs if they're all waiters?"

"Very simple. The workers got together and

"The Brains," a cartoon by Thomas Nast

decided that it wasn't fair for just one or two people to cook the food and others to be cashiers, etcetera, etcetera. They claimed they got bored doing just one job and that they weren't learning anything new. So they decided to rotate all the jobs. Now all the workers do everything: they take turns thinking up the meals, ordering the food, cooking the food, waiting on tables, cleaning up. Why, they decided that one of them would get paid to read magazine articles to the others while the food is being fixed. They said they wanted to talk and learn as they worked."

Taylor, so stunned that he forgot how hungry

he was, shouted, "That's incredible! That is ridiculous! They expect to be paid for learning?! You're running a hamburger joint, not a college!"

The owner nodded sheepishly. "I know. They have gone too far. They are always doing things without asking my permission. I'm ashamed to admit that I don't even know how they make a hamburger—or a milkshake. Look, it's my restaurant, I own it. I want to manage it. I mean, I *am* the boss." The owner's eyes were getting watery. He sat pouting.

"Look here," Taylor said sternly. "Your troubles are at an end. Your little difficulties are nothing compared to what my great-great-grandfather faced. With his three-part scientific management system, I could get you back in control of your workers and your restaurant and keep your profits high. Of course, I must be paid for my services, but it will be worth it."

"Well, at this point, anything is worth a try, Mr. Taylor."

"Hah! That's the fighting spirit! Now let's get down to work."

Taylor began implementing his three-part scientific management system (as he called it).

Stage one was "gathering together all of the traditional knowledge" that the workers had.

Here are the notes Taylor took while making his initial observations:

—In the production of hamburgers, the same person takes a large piece of meat out of a refrigerated room, grinds it up (cutting fat off!), makes it into patties, and cooks it, apparently using whatever spices are his/her favorites—very inefficient.

—Workers also get together to decide which different specials to offer and when to offer them. They determine the price.

—Same worker who makes hamburgers also makes milkshakes—and the ice cream to go into the milkshake (from scratch). (All the ice cream I tasted was good, but the flavor varied slightly depending on which worker made it.) When I asked why they all made hamburgers, ice cream, and milkshakes, workers said they enjoyed the variety.

—Different workers took different amounts of time to make burgers, shakes, etc. There is no set standard. (*Note:* They weren't very cooperative when I arrived in the kitchen with my stop watch. I shan't repeat what one worker called me. One girl said they'd have to vote on whether or not I could be there. The nerve.)

—Owner was right: workers take turns reading newspaper and magazine articles to each other in the kitchen as work is going on. Sometimes they even stop work (!) to discuss a point or tell a story. (Things are worse than I thought.)

—Workers got together and raised the price of french fries and lowered the price of salads. (They told me they wanted to encourage healthier eating habits. Will wonders never cease?)

—Workers do their own bookkeeping to decide what prices to charge and what percentage profits to make. (Surprisingly, the operation is indeed profitable.)

—Workers change decor regularly.

—Workers determine their own hours—they talk out what their needs are and decide on this basis. They also have provided for one another to take maternity leaves and other personal time off (permission of owner not asked).

—Workers wear no uniforms—wear their own clothes—appear to be clean but dressed too much like customers.

—Workers hold their meetings on the premises (often on company time). They have begun talking about turning a back room into a neighborhood day-care center and having cultural events for the neighborhood in the restaurant—all without getting permission from the owner.

Taylor was nervous. What had he gotten himself into? "Sure," he thought, "great-great-grandfather Taylor had applied his scientific management system to making steel—even automobiles. But restaurant work? Goodness, what would F.W. have to say?"

Assignment

It's time for you to help out Taylor IV—even if you don't agree with what he wants to accomplish. He's made an effort to put stage one into practice: collecting all the information about the workplace and the process of producing food at the All-American Deluxe Hamburger Shoppe.

Now he needs to make some recommendations about how the owner can take charge of his restaurant—keeping all the *brainwork* for management and assigning specific tasks to the workers. Feel free to refer to **Student Handout #4: Frederick W. Taylor: Taylorisms.**

Here are some areas for you to consider in helping out Taylor IV:

(1) How should you change the actual process of making food? If you need to learn more about this process, what more do you need to know and how will you go about finding out?

(2) How should you change the way decisions are made? (Examples: pricing, work schedules, work assignments, kinds of food sold, etc.).

(3) Should employees be forced to change the kinds of clothes they wear at work? What *should* employees wear?

(4) How would you change the decor of the hamburger shop?

STUDENT HANDOUT #7-B

CONFESSIONS OF A FRENCH-FRY CHAMPION
by Jeff Edmundson

When I got a job at McDonald's, I thought, "Gee, I'm going to learn how to be a short-order cook." I was wrong. What I learned instead was to churn out large quantities of a few kinds of food by obeying the orders of machines. I might as well have been assembling cars.

I was a high school student, like most of the employees: unskilled, wanting some spending money, and not expecting to be treated any better than I was in school. I started at minimum wage (then, $1.65). Few of us ever got far above that meager floor.

On my first day, I was promptly outfitted in the uniform—a blue smock with the logo and a paper hat. My first training was as a counter person. I was taught the strict six-step procedure, including the exact words with which to greet and leave the customer. I learned how to mark the order on the computer card, and ring up the sale by putting the card in the computer register, which did the rest of the work. (I couldn't be trusted to figure the change due.) I learned to assemble the food in a specified order (drinks, burgers, fries), being careful to put exactly 6–8 pieces of ice in the drinks. I learned to smile a lot, and always to look busy, even if that meant wiping the counter down for the tenth time. This instruction required about half an hour.

I saw quickly that the counter was "women's work." Most of the female employees worked here—where they began, with little hope of leaving. I didn't like all that smiling, and I wanted to be where the action was—on the grill. This was the most skilled position, and as such had the highest status (though not any higher pay). So I set out to climb the career ladder toward that lofty goal.

The first step was the french-fry station.

Now here was a man's job. Fries, as with all food at McDonald's, come preprocessed and frozen. So the first step was to unload a large box of fries by measuring them into metal cooking baskets. When a need for fries was anticipated, usually by a counter person saying, "Damn it, where are my fries?" I dropped a basket into the hot grease and pressed a button. When the buzzer rang, I pulled the basket out, let it drip for exactly thirty seconds, dumped the fries in the tray and shook exactly three shakes of salt onto the pile. Then I slipped a bag onto the specially designed scoop and dropped in the defined number of fries. The bags started looking rather skimpy, so I added a few more to plump them up. The next thing I knew, an angry manager had plopped a scale in front of me and demanded I weigh every bag until I got it right.

From fries it was a short step up to shakes. Once again, this job went to men—mainly to lift and dump the heavy containers of shake mix into the machine which froze the mix. I learned to feed the correct amount of mix into the cup, squirt two squirts of the desired flavor syrup, and stick the cup on the mixing machine, which automatically started when the cup went on.

It actually took me a week to become proficient at these stations—proficiency defined as keeping the machines fed during busy times. It took a week because I was only working two or three hours a night—though not so I could rush home to finish my homework. Rather, like most other employees, I was sent home soon after the dinner rush. This is one of the tricks that makes McDonald's so profitable—never have more workers than necessary. I was going all the way to work and earning the princely sum of $3.30—before taxes.

Ambitious to succeed, I yearned for the chance to reach the peak: the grill. In the meantime, I strove to be the fastest fry-and-shake person around, and was proud to boast that I could run both stations by myself in the busiest hours, for which feat of self-exploitation I was of course richly rewarded with a five-cent raise.

Finally, I made it to the grill. This is the most complicated station, and it took a couple weeks to become good at it. "Good" means fast. At the grill I learned to lay out six frozen patties at a time, like dealing cards. The wide grill could accommodate forty-eight small patties and thirty-six large ones. Buzzers told me when to turn them and when to remove them. At turning, I would sprinkle a specified number of reconstituted onions on each patty.

Meanwhile, someone else put trays of twelve buns into the specially designed toaster, which crisped thirty-six buns every two minutes. The toasted buns were dressed with condiments in squirt guns much like grease guns. Four patties at a time would be laid onto the prepared bottoms, and the twelve tops were neatly dropped on to complete the batch. A good team could put twelve burgers up about every two minutes. (Of great annoyance to us was the customer who deigned to want his burger prepared differ-

ently—the guy who demanded his without mustard. This completely interrupted the timing of our production line, as we singled one patty out for special treatment.)

We passed the burgers over the top of the grill to the warming bin right behind the counter, where they were wrapped. The "bin person" would tell us how many of which kind of sandwich to make. Since this decision required some small measure of judgment, it was also a "high-status" position—and the only one regularly available to women. It was often performed by a manager, otherwise by a senior employee—that is, one who had been around for a few months.

The tremendously high turnover was not a problem for McDonald's, and I suspected managers were actually told to encourage it. New employees, often on their first jobs, were obedient, pliable, and willing to work for almost nothing. And there were certainly few training costs.

Older employees, once they reached the top of the status hierarchy at the grill, tended to become troublemakers. Some of us thought we knew how to run things better than the managers (after all, what kind of people made McDonald's a career?), and even had the arrogance to expect some pay raises. So among many other distractions, McDonald's came up with competitions between stores and workers. Stores competed with each other for cleanliness and friendliness awards, and every year we had competitions between "experts" at various stations. I stumbled happily into this trap, and as a fry whiz won a couple of competitions, entitling me to a cheap medallion and a free dinner.

In a year at McDonald's, my pay never rose above $1.80 an hour. Yet there were only three or four other employees who made as much or more. McDonald's, nonetheless, was successful at creating a measure of employee loyalty. The competitions were a key part of the strategy. These allowed us a kind of "pride" in our work that was otherwise lacking.

Another important weapon was propaganda. Managers constantly "educated" workers in the assorted ways McDonald's was better than the competition, so we were always hearing about the quality of the beef McDonald's bought, or

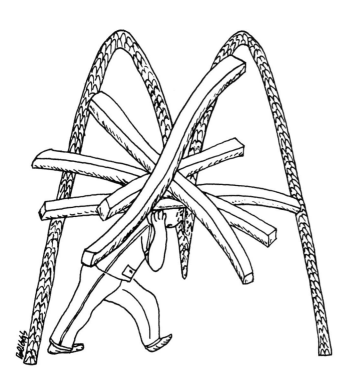

the strict supervision of the shake mix. They even had a little filmstrip projector which showed "we're the greatest" tapes. We believed most of it—we wanted to be proud of what we were doing.

The company also bought our cooperation with the occasional small perk. When we discovered that other McDonald's stores had employee lounges and complained, they walled off a corner of the storeroom and put in a cheap tape player. They threw us a small party once a year. They allowed us to take home leftover food at closing time.

But there were other reasons few of us complained or quit. Most obvious, we were young and didn't know any better. We also knew we weren't going to be at McDonald's forever, so we had little stake in fighting for change. But as important were the friendships we had developed. We knew this at the time and often said we would quit "if it weren't for the people."

While there was competition within the store, it usually remained friendly. Despite the status hierarchy they tried to create, most of us knew we were about the same (though we felt better than the short-time employees). And there we were, high school kids doing something real, working as an efficient team. It made for a pretty high degree of camaraderie.

It's not surprising that unionizing never occurred to us. Not only were we content with the social situation, we were never taught in school that we could organize unions—unions were history, something they had in the 1930s.

McDonald's was an important part of my education. I learned to arrive on time, do what I was told, be a slave to the machine. Looking back, I'm appalled. The job was low-paid, repetitive, and dead-end—and still I put up with it, even liked it. Could that happy robot have been me?

STUDENT HANDOUT #8-A

THE HOMESTEAD STRIKE

At the outbreak of the strike, there were two different groups of workers in Andrew Carnegie's steel mill in Homestead, Pennsylvania, in 1892.

The 800 *skilled workers* were in the minority at the mill, which employed a total of 3,800 men. They were members of a craft union, the Amalgamated Association of Iron and Steel Workers, which had helped them gain wages ranging from $35 to $70 a week and an eight-hour day. It had also helped them gain an important role in making decisions about their working conditions. Committees of workers in each department decided who did what work and regulated many details of running the plant. Through their knowledge and organization, these committees decided everything, from what materials to use to how to get work done. Most of the skilled workers were native-born Americans whose ancestors came from countries in Northern Europe, especially Great Britain and Germany.

But the great majority of workers at Homestead were *unskilled*. They did the dirty work at the plant: lifting, shoveling, pushing. They worked a twelve-hour day with only two vacation days a year and earned under $10 a week. The union had little interest in organizing these people. Their view was: why bother when we, the *skilled* workers, are the most important part of the process of making steel. They felt their union was powerful enough without the unskilled. Furthermore, most of the unskilled workers were recent immigrants—peasants from Eastern Europe who could barely speak English. Some of the union members realized from their experiences that all workers cooperating together could run the country's industries without the need for bosses. They called their vision a "cooperative commonwealth." Most of the skilled workers, however, did not want to associate with the foreign newcomers.

Still, all the workers had important things in common. The accident rate in the steel mills at that time was tremendous. Deaths and injuries from explosions, burnings, asphyxiation, electric shocks, falls, crushing, and other causes were frequent. Although skilled and unskilled workers lived in different neighborhoods, their houses were often owned by the company. Peo-

"Blast Furnace" by Thomas Hart Benton

ple who opposed management could be evicted without warning. Losing one's job automatically meant losing one's home.

The skilled workers had the union to defend them from the employer; the unskilled did not.

In 1892 the union contract was about to expire. Three years earlier, Carnegie had tried to eliminate the union and failed. To make the maximum profits, he needed to tighten control over the work process. Like other industrialists around the country, Carnegie had begun laying plans to reorganize his steel mill. Complex tasks, until then done by skilled workers, were to be broken down into single motions and divided among lower-paid, unskilled people. Machines were to be brought in. Those troublesome skilled workers would no longer be needed, the union would be eliminated, and productivity and profits would soar.

Carnegie imported a professional union-buster, Henry Clay Frick, to run the Homestead plant and gave him the following policy statement: "There has been forced upon this Firm the question whether its Works are to be run 'Union' or 'Non-Union.' As the vast majority of our employees are Non-Union, the Firm has decided that the minority must give place to the majority. These works, therefore, will be necessarily Non-Union after the expiration of the present agreement. . . . This action is not taken in any spirit of hostility to labor organizations, but every man will see that the Firm cannot run Union and Non-Union. It must be one or the other."

Frick built a twelve-foot-high fence, three miles long, around the entire plant, topped it with barbed wire, and bored holes for guns every twenty-five feet. Then he gave the workers an ultimatum: take a pay cut—even though business was still booming in the steel industry—or the union will be broken. Two days before the old contract was to end, he closed the mill and locked out the workers. In response, the union's advisory committee voted to strike.

The Amalgamated Association of Iron and Steel Workers called a meeting of all the workers at the plant. Their goal: to win the support of the unskilled workers for their strike. If everyone would agree not to work at the mill during the strike, then Frick would have a hard time keeping it running. *But,* if the unskilled went to work as scabs, the strike would be lost.

The big question was: would the unskilled workers support the strike?

Questions

1. Why does Carnegie want to get rid of the union at Homestead?

2. What do the skilled and unskilled workers have in common?

3. What differences are there between these workers?

4. (a) What could the unskilled workers lose from supporting the strike? (b) What could they gain?

5. How can the skilled workers get the unskilled workers to support the strike?

STUDENT HANDOUT #8-B

SKILLED WORKER

You are proud to be a member of the Amalgamated Association of Iron and Steel Workers. With 24,000 members, it is the most powerful craft union in the United States. Nobody pushes around a member of the Amalgamated!

You've worked here in Homestead for about fifteen years. You have a highly skilled job as a puddler in the steel-making process, a skill taught you by your uncle. You generally work an eight-hour day, six days a week. You earn from $35 to $70 a week, depending on the price of steel. (If steel prices go up, your wages go up—when prices go down, wages go down.) But even $35 a week is great compared to what those unskilled workers earn: they make less than $10 a week.

In some ways it's really the skilled workers who run the Homestead works. We say, "Carnegie may know how to make money, but the skilled workers know how to make steel." Even if you don't own the mill, you're proud of the control and independence that skilled workers have. It's your skill and control that keep wages up.

For a lot of reasons you're glad to be an American. For one thing, you speak English, like most people in the country. Sometimes you feel there are about a thousand different languages at Homestead. But mostly you're glad because all the good jobs go to the Americans. If you were an unskilled Hungarian or Rumanian, not only would you have the heaviest, dirtiest job, but you'd live in the most crowded, unsanitary housing. If the unskilled were permitted to join the union, not only might they outnumber you, but they might make it easier for the bosses to lower the wage scale.

Even though you look down on the unskilled foreigners, you depend on them. As a skilled puddler you need unskilled helpers. Homestead is a dangerous place for *everybody*, so all the workers—skilled and unskilled—need to look out for each other. Hundreds of people are killed or injured in the steel industry every year.

You will soon be attending the mass meeting called by the Amalgamated. It will be your job to convince the unskilled workers to support the strike. *At the conclusion of the mass meeting there will be a vote to determine if the unskilled workers will support the strike.*

For the next period of time you will meet with other skilled workers so that you can come up with arguments as to why the unskilled should join the strike. In your discussion, consider the following questions:

(1) What do you have in common with the unskilled workers? What differences are there?

(2) Try to anticipate the doubts the unskilled may have about the strike. What might these feelings be?

(3) What arguments could you give to convince the unskilled to support you?

(4) What changes could you make in your behavior or in your strike plans that might convince skeptical unskilled workers? Think about what you could reasonably offer to persuade them to join you on strike.

STUDENT HANDOUT #8-C

UNSKILLED WORKER

You are an unskilled worker at Andrew Carnegie's Homestead steel works. You have only been in the United States for about four years. In your native village, when times were rough, it was common for different families and different workers to help each other out. As the rough times became more frequent, you and your family left Hungary and came to America, hoping for a better life.

Hearing there was work in the steel mills, you left New York City and headed for Pennsylvania. You had never seen a factory like the one you saw at Homestead: huge and loud, with smoke belching everywhere. And, sure enough, you were hired right away.

For four years you've put up with this life. A work week is six, sometimes seven, days. Most days you work twelve hours, averaging about $.14 an hour. This comes out to a little less than $10 a week!

Though you work for Andrew Carnegie, your immediate boss is really one of the skilled workers at the mill. You are considered his unskilled helper. He is paid a certain amount for every ton of steel he makes—the more steel he makes the more he gets paid. *And* the more he gets paid, the more you get. But when his wages go down, yours go down too.

The skilled workers act superior because they were born in America, speak English, and know more about the technical aspects of the work. They also think of themselves as superior because they're organized into a union. However,

they don't want you to belong. "The union is for us skilled workers" is their attitude. Mostly, you socialize with other Hungarians, rather than with Americans.

But although the skilled workers hold themselves above the unskilled, the work is dangerous for everyone. Hundreds of people are killed or injured in the steel industry each year, so you need to help and watch out for one another while you work.

Your living conditions are bad: two rooms, poor sanitation, not enough money for good food, for nice clothes and furniture or to take vacations or to educate your children. What would you do if you made any *less* money?

Soon you will be attending the mass meeting called by the union. The skilled workers will try to convince you to support the strike. *At the conclusion of the mass meeting there will be a vote to determine if the unskilled workers will support the strike.*

For the next period of time you will meet with other unskilled workers. Talk about your feelings toward the union and the strike. In your discussion, consider the following questions:

(1) What do you have in common with the skilled workers? What differences are there between you?

(2) How could you benefit from supporting the strike? How could you lose? What other pros or cons can you think of?

(3) What questions could you ask of the skilled workers? What demands could you make?

STUDENT HANDOUT #8-D

HOMESTEAD STRIKE
The Outcome

At the mass meeting on June 30, 1892, more than 3,000 of the plant's workers jammed into the Homestead Opera House. After discussion, they overwhelmingly voted to support each other and to strike.

A woman who interviewed some of the participants wrote: "The strike began June 30. The Association, which had been so recently indifferent to the conditions of the day men [unskilled workers], now realized, since many of the latter could be put into the skilled positions, that the strike could not be won without their assistance. A call was thereupon issued for them to strike, and the day men, with everything to lose and almost nothing to gain, went out too, and remained faithful supporters to the end."*

Frick hired a private army of hundreds of armed mercenaries to force the strikers back to work. Local sheriffs' deputies had been unwilling to oppose the strikers. When that army was beaten by the workers, with people killed on both sides, the governor of Pennsylvania sent in the state militia. Upon seeing that the troops were friendly to the workers, the general in charge forbade them to talk with strikers or even to walk in the town unless supervised by an officer. The general wrote, "[The workers] believe the works are theirs quite as much as Carnegie's."

Strikebreakers were brought in from different parts of the country, and gradually production resumed. Often they weren't told of their destination until they arrived; many times they were brought in sealed railroad cars after hav-

_____
*Margaret Byington, *Homestead: The Household of a Mill Town* (New York, 1909–1914), p. 9.

ing signed up to go to other Carnegie plants. A number of these men escaped along the way. Afraid for their own safety or unwilling to take other workers' jobs, forced to live inside the plant and work in poor conditions, some managed to get away after arriving.

Still, the workers stayed out on strike. Legal charges were brought against almost two hundred of them for crimes that included treason against the state of Pennsylvania. Found innocent by juries on one set of charges, they were immediately rearrested and tried for other supposed crimes. Ultimately, no striker was ever found guilty of any charge, but the constant prosecutions took the money they had saved for the strike, demoralized them, and kept their leadership locked up during crucial times.

Carnegie owned other mills and was able to continue to produce and sell steel while the strike went on. Workers in other mills also struck, briefly, in solidarity with the Homestead workers. Nevertheless, after four and a half months the strike was lost. With winter approaching, the strikers were forced to return to work on Frick's terms.

Having beaten the union, it was relatively easy for Carnegie and the rest of the steel corporations to introduce changes in work practices and to bring in new machinery. At Homestead, wages were cut, hours were increased, and the number of workers employed was drastically reduced.

Carnegie and Frick decided to change more than work relations at Homestead. They thought that if they could influence the private lives of the workers in their mills, they would have a more obedient workforce. They did this by encouraging the workers to marry and take on

family responsibilities. Instead of renting houses and thus controlling workers through the threat of eviction, they now would *sell* the houses. Owning a home, workers would be tied to their jobs and would have to keep up house payments.

This was a time when a few corporations came to own many of the steel mills. There were attempts in other mills to strike; however, the union still excluded the unskilled, so the workers seldom agreed to follow the leadership of the skilled. Even when there was solidarity between skilled and unskilled workers in one mill, the corporations were able to shift production to other mills and wait out a strike. Within ten years, Carnegie Steel merged with other corporations to become United States Steel, a company that controlled 60 percent of the entire industry.

Questions

1. Based on the outcome of your role play, does the actual decision of the unskilled workers at Homestead to support the strike surprise you? Why or why not?

2. What are the reasons the strike was not successful? Think of the actions taken by both Frick and the government.

3. (a) As a result of their victory, what changes were Carnegie and Frick able to introduce in the workplace (feel free to use what you know from earlier lessons) and in the community? (b) Why did they want these changes?

STUDENT HANDOUT #9-A

BIRTH OF A RANK-AND-FILE ORGANIZER
by Agnes Nestor

Seemingly spontaneous outbursts of workers are usually the result of years of built-up frustration. Often it is the act of one person or a group of persons that sparks a walkout leading to a strike. In this selection Agnes Nestor gives us a picture of both the conditions in the shops and how the glove-making shop in which she was working became unionized. Nestor later became the vice-president of the International Glove Workers Union and president of the Chicago Women's Trade Union League.

Our machines were on long tables in large rooms, and we operators sat on both sides of the tables. At last I was where I had longed to be, and here I worked for ten years. I was earning fairly good pay for those times, and I was happy. We would mark out the quantity of our work and keep account of our earnings. I still have that little book in which I kept my accounts. It is interesting to see how I gradually increased my weekly pay.

To drown the monotony of work, we used to sing. This was allowed because the foreman could see that the rhythm kept us going at high speed. We sang *A Bicycle Built for Two* and other popular songs.

Before we began to sing we used to talk very loudly so as to be heard above the roar of the machines. We knew we must not stop our work just to hear what someone was saying; to stop work even for a minute meant a reduction in pay.

We did want to do a little talking, though. In order not to lose time by it, we worked out a plan. We all chipped in and bought a dollar alarm clock which we hung on the wall. We figured that we could do a dozen pairs of gloves in an hour. That meant five minutes for a pair.

As we worked we could watch the clock to see if we were on schedule. If we saw ourselves falling behind, we could rush to catch up with our own time. No one was watching us or pushing us for production. It was our strategem for getting the most out of the piecework system. We wanted to earn as much as we possibly could.

But, though we all seemed happy at first, gradually it dawned dimly within us that we were not beating the piecework system; it was beating us. There were always "pacemakers," a few girls who could work faster than the rest, and they were the ones to get the new work before the price was set.* Their rate of work had to be the rate for all of us, if we were to earn a decent wage. It kept us tensed to continual hurry.

Also, there were some unjust practices, outgrowths from another era, which nettled us because they whittled away at our weekly pay. We were charged $.50 a week for the power furnished our machines. At first we were tolerant of the charge and called it "our machine rent." But after a time that check-off of $.50 from our weekly pay made us indignant.

We were obliged, besides, to buy our own needles. If you broke one, you were charged for a new one to replace it. We had, also, to buy our own machine oil. It was expensive; and to make matters worse, we had to go to certain out-of-the-way places to obtain it.

But this was not all. Every time a new foreman came in, he demonstrated his authority by inaugurating a new set of petty rules which seemed designed merely to irritate us. One

---

*The price changed at random and often varied from day to day.—*Editor's note.*

such rule was that no girl must leave her own sewing room at noon to eat lunch with a girl in another room. My sister Mary had now come into the factory, and we were in the habit of grouping at lunch time with friends from other departments. But even two sisters from different departments were not permitted to eat lunch together. Mary was in a different department at the time, and this regulation seemed too ridiculous to be borne. Consequently, whenever the foreman had left the room at noon, we went where we pleased to eat our lunch. Sometimes he spied on us and ordered us "Back where you belong!"

In the face of all this, any new method which the company sought to put into effect and disturb our work routine seemed to inflame the deep indignation already burning inside us. Thus, when a procedure was suggested for subdividing our work, so that each operator would do a smaller part of each glove, and thus perhaps increase the overall production—but also increase the monotony of the work, and perhaps also decrease our rate of pay—we began to think of fighting back.

The management evidently heard the rumblings of a threatened revolt. Our department was the "glove-closers." A representative of the company sent for a group from another department, the "banders," asking them to give this new method of subdividing the work a trial and promising an adjustment if the workers' earnings were found to be reduced. The group agreed to try out the new method; but when they got back to their department and told the banders about it, the banders revolted, refused to work the new way on trial, and walked out.

We of our department felt that we should be loyal to the girls who had walked out, and we told the foreman that if the company tried to put new girls in the places of the banders, we would walk out, too!

We had taken a bold step. Almost with spontaneity we had acted in support of one another. Now we all felt tremulous, vulnerable, exposed. With no regular organization, without even a qualified spokesman, how long would such unified action last? If anyone ever needed the protection of a firm organization, I for one at that moment felt keenly that we certainly did.

The glove-cutters, all men, had a union that had existed for about a year. The girl who sat next to me told me about it. She had a boyfriend in this union, but she was always careful not to let anyone hear her talk about it because in those days unions were taboo. She said that the cutters—all men—had talked of trying to get the girls to join the union and had wanted to approach our plant to suggest it, but that some of the members had said, "You'll never get those girls to join a union. They'll stand for anything up there!"

The banders had been smart. They had walked out on Saturday. One of their number decided to get publicity about their grievances and she gave the newspapers the full story about their strike.

The Chicago Federation of Labor was having a meeting that day, and the glove-cutters from our shop had special delegates there. A labor reporter went to these delegates asking for details about the walkout of the banders. It was the first the delegates had heard of the matter. But, learning that the banders of their own factory had struck, they decided to try to get all the girls to join the union.

On Monday the president of the union tried to arrange a meeting with our group. But it was too late. During the weekend, the boss had decided to abandon the new system. Workers had been sent word to come back and everything would be all right, that they could work as before. We felt that now we had a certain power and were delighted over what seemed to us a moral victory. Monday morning found us back at work.

All was not settled, however. On Monday the glove-cutters' union rented a hall within a block of the factory. As we came out from work that afternoon, members of the glove-cutters' union met us, telling us to go to a union meeting at this hall.

Israel Solon was one of these men. Sometimes, if a girl hesitated about going to the hall, he would urge: "Don't be afraid of the boss; protect yourself! Go to the union meeting!"

I was only too anxious to go and did not care who saw me. It seemed legitimate to protect one's self from unjust rules. I went without hesitation.

The meeting was a great success; workers packed the hall, and many nonmembers signed for membership. The work of organizing continued for three evenings, until most of the shop had been persuaded to join.

Toward the end of the week, there was a disturbance in the cutting department. It leaked through to us that a cutter had been discharged and that the cutters were organizing a protest strike. We were young and inexperienced in union procedure; and, as I look back now, I see that because of that lack of experience, and because we were newly organized and therefore anxious to use our new organization, we did a rash thing. We started a strike movement in protest at the discharge of the cutter and also for the redress of our own grievances. We even celebrated the event with a birthday party for one of our girls and had a feast with lemon cream pie at lunch time. During the feast we formulated our plan. We decided it would be cowardly to walk out at noon. We would wait until the whistle blew for us to resume work,

and then, as the power started up on the machines, we would begin our exodus.

Somehow the foreman got wind of our plan. We were forming a line when reinforcements from the foremen's division scattered around the room ordering us to go back to our places. We began to chant: "We are not going to pay rent for our machines!" We repeated it over and over, for that was our chief grievance. . . .

We walked out. We did not use the near-by stairs but walked through the next room in order that the girls there might see us leaving. The girls there were busily at work, quite unconscious of our strike movement. I knew that our cause was lost unless we got those girls to join us. When we got out to the street, I told my companions that all was lost unless we could get those others to walk out too. We lined up across the street shouting "Come on out!" and calling out the names of some of the girls. We kept this up until a few did obey us. Gradually others followed until the shop was almost emptied. Then we paraded to the hall on Leavitt

Street for the meeting with the union leaders.

At the meeting we were called upon to state our demands. We gave them: no more machine rent; no paying for needles; free machine oil; union shop; raises for the cutters who were paid the lowest wages. . . .

Evidently the union officers thought I was a ringleader, for when the committee was appointed to represent our group, my name was called. When Mary heard it, she said: "Why did they put Agnes on? She can't talk!"

This seems amusing to me now; also to certain of my friends who were present at that meeting, for they assure me that I have been talking ever since. . . .

We joined the picket line again and held meetings every day and evening in the hall the cutters had rented. How important we felt! Speakers sent to our evening meetings were furnished by the Chicago Federation of Labor organization committee headed by John Fitzpatrick. One evening they sent Sophie Becker of the Boot and Shoe Workers Union, the only woman on the organization committee. I am afraid that I was a great hero-worshipper in those days! I was so thrilled with her speech that as she left the hall I leaned over just to touch her. Then I leaned back satisfied because I had got that close to her.

All this was happening at the same time that streetcar conductors were being discharged because it became known that they were forming a union. Some of the conductors, as they passed our picket line, would throw us handsful of buttons which read: "ORGANIZE. I'M WITH YOU!"

We wore those buttons on our coats, and when we boarded the cars we would watch the expression on each conductor's face to find out whether or not he had joined the union. . . .

The second week of our strike began. About the middle of the week, we girls on the picket line each received a letter from the company urging us to come back to work and promising that if we reported upon receipt of the letter our old places would be restored to us, that there would be no more machine rent or "power charge," as they called it, that needles would be furnished at cost, that machine oil would be furnished free, and that the cutters would receive a dollar a week raise. But no mention was made of our demand for a union shop. . . .

From Agnes Nestor, "I Become a Striker," *Woman's Labor Leader* (Rockford, Ill.: Bellevue Books, 1954); reprinted in Rosalyn Baxandall, Linda Gordon, and Susan Reverby, eds., *America's Working Women* (New York: Vintage, 1976).

STUDENT HANDOUT #9-B

BIRTH OF A RANK-AND-FILE ORGANIZER
The Conclusion

We talked it all over with misgivings, lest some of the girls be misled by these promises. Without company recognition of our union, we might all be lured back to work, the more progressive and outspoken of us discharged one by one, and all the old practices put back in force, perhaps even more tightly than ever. Such things had happened before. Our safety and our future, we knew, lay in our union. We decided not to return to work just yet. Meanwhile we doubled our picket line, determined that none of our group should falter.

We had hoped to get all the girls in the factory into our union, but we had trouble with the girls of the kid glove department. Only a few of these "aristocrats" had ventured to walk out with us. The rest had remained aloof. Like the gloves they made, the kid glove makers felt that they were superior to the rest of us and used to refer haughtily to the rest of us as the "horsehide girls."

During one of the last days of our strike, one of these kid glove girls passed along our picket line on her way to work. We told her that she wasn't going in; we formed a circle around her and took her to the streetcar a block away and waited to see that she went home. We stood waiting for the car beside a long water trough where teamsters watered their horses. One girl who was holding tightly to the kid glove maker threatened, "Before I let go of you, I will duck you in that water trough." It was only an idle threat; of course she did not intend doing it.

Newspapermen were on hand trying to get stories about the strike. Luke Grant, a veteran labor reporter, was watching as we put the girl on the streetcar.

Next morning a front-page story appeared headlined, "STRIKERS DUCK GIRL IN WATER TROUGH." Other newspapers carried the same fiction and played it up for several days, some even with cartoons of the fictitious event. . . .

Perhaps because of this newspaper publicity—Luke Grant always insisted that his story won the day for us—or perhaps because it looked as though we girls would refuse forever to return to work unless all our demands were met, the management agreed to our union shop and to the redress of all our grievances. We went back to work the following Monday with, as we said, "flying colors." Our union shop, we felt, was our most important gain.

STUDENT HANDOUT #10-A

YOU ARE IN THE IWW

The year is 1912. New industries, based on new kinds of machinery, new ways of organizing work, and a greater use of unskilled and foreign-born workers, are flourishing. Most established labor unions (such as those in the American Federation of Labor or AFL) have not tried to organize these unskilled workers. But one has: the Industrial Workers of the World, the IWW. You are a member of this union.

You feel strongly that the IWW is the only union with a future because it understands what's really going on in this country. As you see it, the other major labor federation, the AFL, is living in the past. It was born in an era when most production was done by craftsmen owning their own hand tools—each trade was difficult and required lots of skill and time to learn. When there was conflict between skilled workers and owners, the craftsmen got together and formed trade unions to protect themselves. These were unions based on a particular craft—shoemakers, carpenters, bricklayers, and the like.

But times have changed. Industry in the United States has been revolutionized. The hand tool has almost disappeared. Instead, there are huge factories with machines run by workers who don't own their own tools and have little control over how the work is performed. Ownership has changed also. Now, an individual factory may be only one of many controlled by the same owners. Yet the AFL craft unions continue as if nothing has changed—they still organize craft by craft. In your view, this divides the workers and lets the owners play one craft or one factory against another. For instance, when workers in one factory go on strike, the owners simply step up production elsewhere.

The IWW, on the other hand, believes in the idea of One Big Union. And you think that the IWW is right: all workers—skilled and unskilled, native-born and foreign-born, men and women—should be in the same union. In your mind, it's time to stop this nonsense of organizing only skilled, American-born men. You like what Big Bill Haywood—one of the most famous IWW members—says: "The AFL organizes like this"—separating his fingers as far apart as they can go, and naming the separate crafts. "The IWW organizes like this"—making a tight fist and shaking it at the bosses.

There are other important differences between the IWW and the AFL craft unions. The AFL just wants a little bigger piece of the pie. As one AFL leaders puts it, "There is no belief in the AFL trade unions that its members shall control the factory or take away the rights of owners. We have no ultimate ends. We are going on from day to day. We are fighting only for immediate objects—objects that can be realized in a few years." Higher wages, shorter hours, improved conditions—that's all the AFL is after.

You IWW members see these goals as short-sighted. As far as you are concerned, the problems of working people will only begin to be solved when workers take over all the workplaces and run them *collectively* for the benefit of the whole society—not just for the private profit of the owners. As long as owners run industry for their own profit, there will be continual conflict between them and the workers they control. You believe that all wealth is produced by the workers, so all wealth should be controlled by the workers—what do owners produce?

Thus, *the goal of the IWW is not only for higher wages or shorter hours, but to change the whole society.* Workplaces and *all* of society should be run by the people who produce, the people who do the work.

At first when you heard IWW members talking like this you thought it was a little silly. "They're dreaming," you said to yourself. "What do workers know about running anything, much less a factory or the whole society!"

However, as you came to know the IWW folks better, you saw they run their organization in a way that actually *teaches* people to be leaders and thinkers. The IWW halls you've visited have good libraries on economics and social questions. Workers hold classes to teach one another. They put on plays and sing together. Most importantly, the IWW also insists that all the members participate in making decisions in the organization.

The AFL seems to be afraid of strikes. The IWW isn't. What better learning experience could there be than a confrontation between capitalists and workers? A strike allows the IWW to illustrate to workers that, "The capitalist class and the working class have nothing in common." Strikes are an important opportunity for deepening workers' understanding that they can trust each other and for making important decisions together.

The IWW is more than an organization, it's a way of life. You want to convince other workers that it's the *right* way of life. One of the slogans of the IWW is, "We must form the structure of the new society in the shell of the old." That is a goal you've come to believe in.

You in the IWW don't believe in the idea of "follow the leader." That might be the way it is in *this* society, but it's not the way you want it to be in the *new* society. Your goal is for every union member to be a "leader."

Recently, you read a speech by a famous IWW member, Eugene Debs. Debs summed up the IWW belief: "The average workingman imagines that he must have a leader to look to; a guide to follow, right or wrong. He has been taught in the craft union that he is a very dependent creature; that without a leader the goblins would get him without a doubt, and he therefore instinctively looks to his leader. You have depended too much on that leader and not enough on yourself. I don't want you to follow me. I want you to cultivate self-reliance. If I have the slightest capacity for leadership I can only give evidence of it by 'leading' you to rely on yourselves."

That's what democracy is all about as far as you're concerned: everyone a leader, a thinker, a participant.

You Are in the IWW: Membership Questions

1. As an IWW member, what do you think are the most significant differences between the IWW and the AFL? List these as a chart on a separate sheet of paper or on the reverse side of this page.

2. What would other members of the IWW have thought of the actions you personally took in the **Organic Goodie** simulation? Explain.

3. How would AFL members have reacted? Explain.

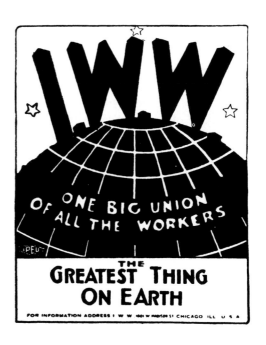

STUDENT HANDOUT #10-B

LAWRENCE, 1912—PART 1
The Strike Is On!

Work conditions in Lawrence, Massachusetts, were undergoing the same kinds of changes that were occurring in industries across the United States. In the mid-nineteenth century, Lawrence had been a pleasant place to work. Young farm women labored in the new textile mills. They lived with chaperones in company housing, gave concerts for each other, and wrote literary journals.

Then, in the 1880s, the mill owners introduced new technology. They brought in new machinery and lowered wages. They began to recruit immigrants from Europe. At first, they brought in just one nationality; then, to keep the workforce divided, another and another. To make the work seem attractive, they sent postcards to different parts of Europe that showed workers leaving the mills carrying bags of money on their way to the bank.

By 1912, there were dozens of different ethnic groups in Lawrence, speaking almost thirty different languages: Italian and Polish, Ukrainian and Yiddish, Portuguese and French. This Massachusetts city now produced more cloth than any other city in the country. And yet workers often couldn't afford to buy jackets. Malnutrition was common. Housing was crowded and lacking in light and sanitation. The life expectancy of a Lawrence *worker* was twenty-two years less than that of a factory *owner*. Because of low wages, entire families had to work in the mills. Of the more than 30,000 workers, half were in their teens. In fact, one-half of the children in Lawrence between fourteen and eighteen years old worked in the mills. A small percentage of the workers had better paid, skilled jobs. The AFL craft union had 208 members. It did not have a contract with the owners.

Not one of the mill owners lived in Lawrence. Profits were rising, and the pace of work was continually increasing. In 1905, the owners decided that each worker in the woolen mills would operate two looms instead of one. In the cotton mills, every worker now tended twelve different machines at once.

To speed up production, supervisors had arbitrary authority to fire people. Women workers were pressured to date and provide sexual favors to their foremen. Foremen were openly abusive and disrespectful to the foreign-born workers. Water in the mills was so contaminated by the heat and dust that it was undrinkable. Supervisors had bottled water available for sale. Part of the wages were paid on what was called the "premium system." This meant that any worker who was sick for more than one day in the month, or failed to produce the amount set by the supervisor (because his or her machine broke, for instance), lost the premium. Since skilled workers received their premium according to the production of the unskilled workers under them, they also put pressure on them and played favorites.

The usual work week was fifty-six hours. Concerned about health conditions, the state legislature passed a law that limited work hours for children and women to fifty-four hours (six days a week, nine hours a day). Immediately, the owners saw a way to take advantage of this reform. They sped up the work yet again, so that the same amount of cloth was produced in fifty-four hours as had been produced in fifty-six.

Now the question was: would the workers' pay checks be lowered? Since housing costs weren't going down, any pay cut would simply mean less to eat. On January 12, workers opened their pay envelopes to find . . . a pay cut.

"Bell Time" by Winslow Homer

After a few stunned seconds, in desperation, someone yelled "Strike!"

The strike spread quickly. Within days, more than 20,000 workers were picketing, often singing as they marched.

The national president of the AFL union came to Lawrence to try to discourage the strike. He was even more harsh than management in criticizing the strikers. His members—generally American-born skilled workers—crossed the picket lines and continued to work. The union president's tactic was to demonstrate his loyalty to management in hopes of being rewarded with union recognition. He offered a deal to the mill owners: sign a contract with his union and the AFL would continue to oppose the strike. Confident of victory, and opposing unions in any form, management refused.

After about three weeks the strike was so effective that there remained little work for the skilled workers. Then they too joined the strike. Thousands of strikers became members of the Industrial Workers of the World—the IWW.

STUDENT HANDOUT #10-C

LAWRENCE PROBLEM SOLVING #1
Getting Organized

1. There are a number of different mills in Lawrence on strike. This involves over 30,000 workers. Many different ethnic groups are represented in Lawrence. Lots of different languages are spoken and there are a number of cultures in the city.

   Question: **How is the strike going to be "led"? Who will decide how to negotiate, what the demands of the strike should be, what tactics to use, whether to end the strike, etc.?**

2. Many of the workers in Lawrence are illiterate. People speak a number of different languages. There are thousands of people involved in the strike, in more than one factory.

   Question: **Specifically, what kind of "organizational structure" should we use throughout the strike? (Some possibilities: large meetings involving all the strikers, elected representatives, rotating leadership, some other method.)**

3. *Question:* **How should any meetings we hold be run? By whom?**

4. *Question:* **How can we make sure that we keep the strikers unified?**

5. With the thugs hired by management, the picket line can be dangerous and some people feel that it is no place for a woman. These workers help support this position by pointing out that women are not even allowed to vote in national or local elections. Remember, the year is 1912.

   Question: **Should women be allowed to participate in the strike? If so, in what capacity?**

6. There have been charges in the newspapers that some of the strikers are "illegal immigrants" who came to this country only in order to send money home.

   Question: **What should we do about these people?**

STUDENT HANDOUT #10-D

LAWRENCE, 1912—PART 2
Unity in Diversity

An outdoor meeting of thousands of strikers—men, women, and children—discussed and then agreed on the demands of the strike. People would not return to work until four conditions were met:

(1) A wage increase

(2) Extra pay for working overtime

(3) An end to the premium system of payment and the pressures it brought

(4) No penalties or discrimination against strikers

Each day, there were mass meetings organized according to nationality—Hungarians met with Hungarians, Italians with Italians, etc. These were the major decision-making meetings, chaired by people elected from the group. Here delegates reported to the strikers and received further directions from them.

A strike committee met every morning to coordinate activities. It consisted of elected delegates, four from each of fourteen nationality groups, fifty-six in all, covering every workplace and every type of job. Delegates could be replaced at any time by the group that elected them. A second committee of fifty-six served as a back-up in case members of the strike committee were arrested. Delegates met outdoors so that their discussions could be heard and evaluated by everyone. In these gatherings the many strikers who attended could gain a renewed sense of their own numbers and strength.

On Saturdays and Sundays, huge meetings brought everyone together, tens of thousands of strikers and their families. At these and at the daily ethnic group meetings, there was entertainment, in addition to reports and discussions. People sang together, danced, and enjoyed performances by their neighbors.

These were meetings for all strikers, whether or not they were IWW members. In addition, the IWW called special meetings for women and children to encourage their participation and leadership. Organizers talked extensively with husbands to overcome their resistance to wives speaking in public or marching on the picket lines. In the difficult conditions of the strike, people discovered many new abilities: chairing meetings, speaking out publicly, organizing committees.

There were numerous efforts to divide the strikers. Newspapers and some religious leaders criticized husbands for permitting their wives and daughters to play an active role. Attempts were made to pit ethnic groups against each other. Some priests told Irish workers, for instance, that they were superior to the non-English-speaking nationalities. City officials charged that some of the workers were "illegal immigrants" and should be deported. These efforts took their toll. Some husbands kept their wives at home. Some nationalities participated more actively than did others. Overwhelmingly, however, the strikers remained firm, maintaining a belief that everyone had a right to work in decent conditions and to develop fully his or her leadership capabilities.

STUDENT HANDOUT #10-E

BREAD AND ROSES

As we come marching, marching in the beauty of the day,
A million darkened kitchens, a thousand mill lofts gray,
Are touched with all the radiance that a sudden sun discloses,
For the people hear us singing: "Bread and roses! Bread and roses!"

As we come marching, marching, we battle too for men,
For they are women's children, and we mother them again.
Our lives shall not be sweated from birth until life closes;
Hearts starve as well as bodies; give us bread, but give us roses!

As we come marching, marching, unnumbered women dead
Go crying through our singing their ancient cry for bread.
Small art and love and beauty their drudging spirits knew.
Yes, it is bread we fight for—but we fight for roses, too.

As we come marching, marching, we bring the greater days.
The rising of the women means the rising of the race.
No more the drudge and idler—ten that toil where one reposes,
But a sharing of life's glories: Bread and roses! Bread and roses!

(Written by James Oppenheim)

Questions

1. What is meant by "bread" in the song?

2. What is meant by "roses"?

3. Give examples of what might satisfy the demand for "roses."

4. Are the "roses" mainly of concern to women or to men also?

5. "The rising of the women means the rising of the race." What are the different possible meanings of "rising" in that sentence? What is the "race" to which the song refers?

6. What will enable the "sharing of life's glories" in the fourth verse?

STUDENT HANDOUT #10-F

LAWRENCE PROBLEM SOLVING #2
Can We Win?

1. Early in the strike, without meeting with any of the strikers, the employers agree to restore the fifty-six-hour pay rate. If we don't go back to work, they may withdraw that decision.

   Question: Shall we claim victory and go back to work? If not, what *should* we do?

2. The commanding officer of the militia that has been sent to Lawrence insists that different groups of strikers meet separately with each employer. His hope is that agreements will be reached with some employers and that some groups of strikers will be able to return to work.

   Question: How do we respond?

3. Our strike committee has just traveled to Boston for a meeting with the president of the largest group of mills. No agreement was reached. But now false reports are being circulated and newspapers are announcing that a settlement was reached and that the strike is over. Tomorrow is Monday. We know that employers are gearing up to reopen the mills. If people believe the rumors and return to work, the strike will be lost.

   Question: What can we do?

4. There are still some people crossing the picket lines. Some of them are showing up at the relief committees while continuing to work.

   Question: Should we feed them?

5. Violence has been increasing. Two people have been killed. While picketing, a woman was shot by a policeman. A boy was bayoneted in the back while fleeing the militia. Our people are scared. Some want to end the violence by returning to work. Others are becoming restless and want to fight back with violence.

   Question: **What should we tell both groups?**

6. (a) Because of the violence, some of us fear for the safety of our children. Not only that, our resources here are limited and the children are hungrier than usual.

   Question: **What can we do? What should we tell our children?**

   (b) Having members from so many different backgrounds means we can learn from each other's experiences and traditions. One group has said that during a bitter strike in their country, children are sometimes sent to the homes of workers in other cities. We have many supporters in New York City and elsewhere.

   Question: **Is this something we should do? If we send the children, is there some way they can win even greater support for our strike?**

7. Martial law has been declared. All picketing is forbidden, as is any gathering of more than two people on the street.

   Question: **How can we respond? (Without picketing and meeting, our strike will die.)**

8. A "Citizens Association" has been formed by local merchants and city officials against "outside agitators." "After all," they say, "our own good Lawrence folk wouldn't dream of striking." A "God-and-Country" campaign has been launched by the mayor. Businesses are flying American flags, citizens are being encouraged to wear patriotic lapel pins, all directed against the IWW. We too love the country, but we certainly have a different vision of what it should become. We also have 14,000 members now in Lawrence.

   Question: **How can we respond?**

STUDENT HANDOUT #10-G

LAWRENCE, 1912—PART 3
The Outcome

Pressures and Response

As the strike continued, one of the employers' tactics was to try to undermine worker solidarity. Not too long after the strikers agreed on all four demands, the employers posted notices that they were restoring the former wages. For fifty-four hours' work (but fifty-six hours worth of production because of speedup), workers were to receive the same amount they had been paid for working fifty-six hours. If a significant number accepted this offer and returned to the mills, the strike would have been broken.

Many workers must have been tempted. They were not used to challenging authority. Living conditions while on strike were difficult. However, people remembered that living conditions had also been difficult when they were working. The strike meetings and activities were beginning to give them a sense of their own strength and hope for a better settlement. The strikers held firm.

There were other efforts to divide the strikers or seize the initiative from them. Employers agreed to negotiate, but only on a company-by-company basis, not with the strike committee representing all the strikers. Recognizing that separate negotiations or even settlements with only some of the employees would pull them apart, the strikers refused. An agency of the Massachusetts government intervened. The strike committee agreed to let the agency try to get the employers to sit down with the strikers and negotiate (i.e., to mediate). However, the committee refused to let the agency decide the agenda or what the settlement would be (i.e., to arbitrate).

The strikers fell into a trap. The president of the largest textile company agreed to meet in Boston with representatives from the strike committee. The meeting took place over a weekend and led to no agreement. As strike committee members returned to Lawrence on Sunday, they found that false rumors were being spread, reinforced by newspaper stories, that a settlement had been reached. Supervisors were already gearing up the mills for the next day. The strike committee decided on a rally for very early Monday morning. From the rally thousands of strikers marched in an immense parade, stopping and alerting all the people who had believed the false reports.

Both employers and government continued pressure. Martial law was declared. Twenty-two companies of militia took over the town, including many Harvard boys carrying bayonets "up to teach those workers a lesson." Any gathering of more than two people on the streets was banned, as was the stationing of pickets near the mills.

Strike Tactics

Their use of a parade led the workers on strike to other new tactics. Since the merchants couldn't survive if the order against gathering was enforced downtown, the strikers responded by going to the business district first. They formed large groups, posing as customers, milling in and out of stores but buying nothing. Other customers, of course, were reluctant to shop. The merchants quickly insisted that the authorities withdraw their order against gathering. Then the strikers formed an "endless chain of pickets," 7,000 to 10,000 people, circling the entire industrial district. They maintained this constantly moving picket line for the remaining weeks of the strike.

Keeping up morale was the key to maintaining the strike, so providing for the needs of the strikers and their families was one of the most important tasks of the strikers' organizations. Publicity and finance committees got support from workers all across the country. Relief committees, organized by nationality, distributed food or money for food and fuel to more than 50,000 of the 86,000 people who lived in Lawrence. Some of the people still working tried to sneak in line and get assistance. They were always encouraged to stop crossing the picket lines, and were refused relief if they didn't join the strike. The AFL set up its own relief organization, providing aid only to people who agreed to end their strike.

BAR SHIPMENT OF STRIKE CHILDREN; WOMEN CLUBBED

Youngsters Trampled in Riot When Lawrence Police Halt Exportation.

MOTHERS FIGHT WITH TEETH AND HATPINS

Violence

With so many workers away from their jobs, the authorities continually raised the threat of violence by strikers. As workers left their looms the first day, the municipal government rang the bells of city hall in a riot alarm. The first attempts at picketing outside the mills were met with icy water sprayed from the rooftops by company supervisors. When drenched and freezing workers retaliated by throwing pieces of ice, the police moved in. Those strikers who were caught received ten-minute trials and sentences of a year in jail.

Upon leaving their looms, some of the strikers had cut the belts that transmitted power. During the strike, when some workers continued to cross picket lines, the strikers tried persuasion, pressure, and even intimidation. Years of pent up frustration could have led to disorganized fighting or further attacks on property. Instead, the strikers almost always responded to the IWW call for discipline and peaceful protest.

There were many provocations. Police raids uncovered dynamite and newspapers across the country blamed the strikers. This episode was used as the excuse for closing the industrial district to pickets and for further police harass-

ment. A trial showed that the dynamite had been planted to discredit the strike. A small group of local merchants had hidden the dynamite, then called the police. The conspiracy was planned in textile company offices.

A woman picket was shot and killed. In spite of many witnesses who identified a particular policeman as the killer, police arrested two IWW leaders who were speaking more than a mile away. That morning, streetcars had been stopped and their windows smashed. Strikers identified thugs, hired by the mill owners, as responsible. Police repeatedly attacked picket lines, beating people so severely that pregnant women miscarried. A boy, fleeing the militia, was bayoneted in the back and died.

Because of difficult conditions, the violence, and the shortage of food and fuel, the strikers decided to accept another form of aid. As an expression of solidarity, workers in New York and Philadelphia invited young children of the strikers to come stay with them. The first trainloads of young people were welcomed warmly and also created favorable publicity for the strike. The next time a group of children was taken to the train station in Lawrence, police surrounded the station, then attacked, severely beating the children and their parents. Children and parents were taken to jail and separated. The authorities began proceedings to take the children from their parents permanently.

Victory

Ultimately, the use of violence by the authorities backfired, and the discipline of the strikers prevailed. With families waiting in other cities to receive the children, the train station brutality became international news. A Socialist Party representative began congressional hearings about the situation in Lawrence. The hearings focused not only on the immediate violence, but on the long-term violence of hunger, inadequate clothing and housing, early deaths, and the stunted lives of children.

By now the strike had been going for more than two months. The companies kept the machinery running to make it sound as if they were continuing business as usual, although in fact they had not been able to produce any textiles. More than most industries, the textile companies were vulnerable to public outrage and congressional pressure. Their high profits were based in part on a tariff that kept out foreign textiles and gave the U.S. industry a near-monopoly. Now that their own tactics had risked undermining public support for their tariff, management decided to settle the strike. They asked the strike committee to begin serious negotiations and quickly agreed to all four of the strikers' demands.

A meeting of 15,000 strikers voted to accept the agreement. There would be wage increases, with the greatest increases going to the workers who had been most poorly paid. There would be extra pay for overtime work. No worker would be discriminated against for having been on strike. The premium system would be changed to reduce the pressure, with payment every two weeks instead of once a month.

Strikers returned to work; children came home to their families. The IWW, tiny before the strike, now had 14,000 members in Lawrence. And the struggle continued. The mayor began a "God and Country" campaign, using patriotism to claim the IWW was "un-American." A threatened boycott of "God and Country" merchants by IWW members ended that campaign. Two of the IWW leaders were still in jail on trumped-up murder charges. The IWW declared a political strike in Lawrence. Thousands of workers stayed away from work for a day to protest the continued jailing and to insist on a fair trial. Textile workers in other cities also threatened to strike if the two men were framed. The textile companies fired 1,500 workers for participating in the political strike. They backed down completely, however, rehiring every worker, when the IWW threatened renewed strike action. A jury trial found the IWW leaders not guilty.

Postscript

The Lawrence strikers won a victory that most of the organized labor movement had thought impossible. They united women and men, mainly unskilled workers from dozens of nationality groups. They vastly increased their own self-confidence, skills and knowledge, and built what seemed to be a powerful local union. Yet within the next few years, the union was again reduced to a small group and management succeeded in taking back some of the strikers' gains.

The reasons for this decline are complex. Some of the IWW's most skilled organizers left Lawrence after the strike, to spread the victory and try to build unions elsewhere. There was increased repression nationally against the IWW, with more trials, deportations, and even massacres of supporters. The more important cause, however, was probably what happened in the economy and the ways management took advantage of that. In the periodic recessions of the next few years, the owners were able to lay off workers who had been militant and to lower wages and speed up working conditions. Further, the companies expanded to locations where the workers were not organized. Now they were able to outlast a strike in one location by increasing production in their mills elsewhere.

In the new large-scale industries, militant workers in just one location would have limited strength. Factory- and city-wide organizing efforts were insufficient; the next step would require workers to organize throughout whole industries. Until that happened, indeed long after, the "singing strike" continued to provide inspiration.

Questions

1. Read over **Lawrence, 1912—Part 3: The Outcome.** What are the important similarities between the answers you came up with in class and what the strikers actually decided in Lawrence? What are the important differences?

2. Why do you suppose the IWW lost so many members in Lawrence in the few years after the strike? Could they have done anything differently to preserve and strengthen their influence?

3. From your problem-solving in class, what have you learned about making decisions in groups? For example, why is it so difficult for people in our society to make decisions together? Why don't school systems place a higher priority on teaching these skills? What are good methods of solving problems as a group? etc.

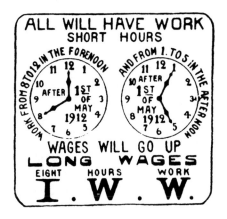

STUDENT HANDOUT #11-A

IT'S A MYSTERY
Clues

In 1910 the black population of Midwest City was 1,800.

In 1920 the black population of Midwest City was 9,000.

Most of the blacks who came to Midwest City between 1910 and 1920 had no previous experience or skills in factory work.

With the production boom of World War I, there was a shortage of workers in Midwest City.

U.S. involvement in World War I ended in November 1918.

There was a severe housing shortage in Midwest City in 1917 and 1918.

When there is competition for scarce housing, rents and prices rise.

Fearing too much competition for their jobs, most unions in Midwest City did not allow unskilled workers to be members.

Before World War I, the black neighborhoods in Midwest City had been quite small.

During World War I, blacks began moving into Midwest City neighborhoods which for some years had housed poor whites.

In several well-known strikes around the country, blacks, unable to get other factory jobs, had been hired as strikebreakers, or "scabs."

Union members feel strongly that when they are out on strike other workers should not take their jobs.

To get most of the higher paying skilled factory jobs in Midwest City, a worker had to be in a union.

Between 1915 and 1916, industrial production in Midwest City increased by over two-thirds.

World War I started in Europe in 1914, but the United States didn't join the war until 1917.

Many of the new black residents in Midwest City seemed different because they came from the South and weren't used to city ways.

During times of high unemployment, people are often afraid of losing their jobs.

Companies often fired workers when they could find other people who were willing to work for lower wages.

Because of the low pay they were used to in the South, blacks in the North were often willing to work for lower wages than other workers.

When blacks were hired in Midwest City factories, they were usually given jobs that kept them separate from whites.

At the end of World War I, war production in Midwest City stopped and many people, black and white, were thrown out of work.

Police in Midwest City reported an increase in crime in 1919.

Many white Midwest City residents returned from World War I looking for jobs and housing.

Many companies sent representatives to the South during World War I looking for people to come to Midwest City to work in their factories.

Most of the new blacks in Midwest City came from the South.

During World War I, many of Midwest City's factories produced war materiel—guns, bullets, even airplanes.

Unemployment was high for all races after the war, but especially for blacks. In all, a total of 15,000 people—as much as a third of the workforce of Midwest City—were looking for jobs.

In an attempt to keep profits high, a number of Midwest City companies lowered wages after World War I.

There were numerous strikes in Midwest City during and after World War I.

After World War I, some companies in Midwest City advertised specifically for "colored laborers."

STUDENT HANDOUT #11-B

IT'S A MYSTERY
Questions

Every good detective needs to use deduction—making general observations from specific facts. Answer the following questions as a group using the clues that you have. *All* clues must be used at least *once* in your answers. Remember—you may say your clue aloud but you may not show it to anyone else.

Questions that are starred are opinion questions. You won't need the clues to answer these.

1. What major changes took place in Midwest City from the period before World War I to after?

2. After World War I, what problems faced Midwest City residents for which whites may have blamed blacks?

3. Are there better explanations for each problem?

4. (a) Why were blacks singled out as scapegoats for many of these problems? (b) Do you think this was fair? Explain.*

5. Did unions benefit or suffer from going along with the discrimination?*

STUDENT HANDOUT #12-A

SOUTHERN TENANT FARMERS' UNION

Time: Early 1935

Place: Augusta, Arkansas

Scene: Two tenant farmers—one black and one white—are discussing the new Southern Tenant Farmers' Union which is being organized in the Arkansas delta. One of the farmers is a member of the union and is traveling around trying to get other farmers to join up. The other farmer is very skeptical, largely because the STFU encourages both blacks and whites to become members. The skeptical farmer doesn't believe blacks and whites can or should work together.

Assignment: Using the information provided below, as well as what you've already studied, write a detailed dialogue between these two tenant farmers. You decide whether the union organizer is black or white.

Background: It is the middle of the Great Depression and farmers, especially those who rent land or are "sharecroppers"—people who use others' land in exchange for part of their crop—are hard hit. For one thing, cotton prices have gone steadily down. The response of the federal government has made matters worse. In 1933 the Agricultural Adjustment Act was passed. The AAA was intended to boost cotton prices by paying farmers to take land out of production. According to the law, no tenant farmers or sharecroppers were *supposed* to be evicted from their farms. But that's not how it has worked. Between 1933 and 1934 an estimated 900,000 people—black and white—have been thrown off the land by plantation owners taking advantage of the AAA.

For many, this action is the final straw and people have begun organizing. Even before the

Depression, conditions for all sharecroppers, tenant farmers, and farmworkers had been bad. Life in the Arkansas delta was controlled by white plantation owners. Many plantations were almost like their own little countries. Payment for work or crops would often be made not in cash but in "script," which could only be spent at the company store. Certain plantations had their own court system, with a justice of the peace appointed by the plantation owner. Some large plantations even had their own penal farms. These conditions still exist.

Small farmers, whether black or white, are almost always in debt to the plantation owners. In order to earn enough to live, many farmers also work as wage laborers on the plantations. A typical wage might be $.35 for 100 pounds of cotton. With hard work, a picker might end up with 300 pounds at the close of the day. However, high prices are charged for the seeds and fertilizer the pickers need for their own farms. It is possible to get by, but with nothing left over.

In a bad year, it is easy for a farmer to lose what little land he has. By 1935, many people on the plantations are "coming down the agricultural ladder." A farmworker's grandfather may have owned his own farm, his father might have been a tenant farmer owning his own team and tools, but the farmworker now has no land and is forced to work solely for wages.

Though times are hard for black and white workers alike, conditions are not identical. For example, schools are segregated and those for blacks are inferior. Black students are allowed to attend school only seven months out of the year. The rest of the time they are expected to work in the fields. White children are in school every day.

Travel is more difficult for blacks. There are

parts of many counties where it still is not safe for blacks to go unless accompanied by a white person.

In the past, blacks were active in trying to change oppressive conditions. But their attempts were brutally repressed. Fifteen years ago, a black sharecroppers' union was ended by the Elaine Massacre. The all-black Alabama Share-croppers' Union had been similarly put down in 1931.

The new Southern Tenant Farmers' Union will be for blacks and whites. But it too is sure to face tough going. Plantation owners have announced that they don't want "niggers" organized. The police, acting on behalf of the owners, have begun arresting white and black organizers. Whites have trouble finding meeting places because the largest halls, the churches, are controlled by the wealthy.

Organizing the Southern Tenant Farmers' Union will be no easy task.

Organizers will encounter attitudes from both blacks and whites that will make building a strong integrated union difficult. The following are a few of the attitudes you will need to deal with in your dialogue:

—Many whites think of themselves as superior to blacks. They are constantly told that they are better because they are white and that they have no use for blacks.

—Blacks have few reasons to trust whites. Many whites treat blacks harshly. Many blacks wonder why the union needs to include whites.

—About 75 percent of the tenant farmers in the delta are black; 85–90 percent of the agricultural laborers are black. Why would white farmers want to be members of a union that will probably be led by blacks?

—Whites have a number of privileges—better schools, unrestricted travel, the right to vote—that blacks are denied. Whites may fear los-

ing their privileges if they organize with blacks. Blacks may feel that whites, with all their privileges, would be unreliable allies.

—Both blacks and whites know about past massacres of union members. They all have reason to be frightened. Why should this time be any different?

Cotton Pickers!
STRIKE!
For $1 per 100 lbs
Refuse to pick a boll for less!

Strike on every farm or plantation where cotton is being picked for wages!

Accept No Less Than The Union Prices—-- $1 per 100 lbs

Strike Call Effective TODAY

Special Committee

SOUTHERN TENANT FARMERS UNION

See Instructions for local strikes Committees

Please Pass This On

STUDENT HANDOUT #12-B

SOUTHERN TENANT FARMERS' UNION
Oral History

Naomi Williams: During the Depression I had a crop of my own. And if I had a little leisure time to get off, I'd go over there to the boss's place and pick cotton. And that was for $.35 a hundred. I was a good cotton picker; and I picked 300 pounds in one day to get me a dollar and a nickel. I'd go out there in the early morning just so you could see a row of cotton. It was hard, but I made it. I tried to keep my own account at the commissary store. But now where the cheating came in was on this stuff you put on the cotton, fertilizer and all that kind of stuff, and in the seeds. When they sell the cotton, they wouldn't give me what the cotton was worth. They put it there and I had to pay it all. I was renting but I wasn't supposed to pay it all. But I had all that to pay. Yes, I owed them at that store everything. I gathered crops so much. And then when I'd get enough crop gathered, then I'd pay him. I had got all my groceries and that would leave me with nothing.

I usually made forty and forty-five bales, more sometimes, and I had enough money to run me through the winter, to buy new children's clothes for school and to buy groceries to last till the next time they start to furnish over in the spring. They didn't never give us nothing until the first of April. But I was wise. I'd buy enough of what I couldn't raise to last till April or May. I was raising hogs, had cows, and made my own garden and put up dry food, beans and peas and all that. I done worked myself to death. . . .

H.L. Mitchell: I have always said that my family came down the agricultural ladder. My father was a tenant farmer who owned his team and farming tools. My grandfather owned his own farm and lived near Halls, Tennessee. He was also a Baptist preacher. From the time I was eight years old I worked for wages on the farm. I worked for $.50 per day upwards. I made my first sharecrop about 1919. . . .

Clay East: The way I remember the union getting started—see, in the South we call twelve o'clock "dinner." When Norman Thomas [the leader of the Socialist Party] was there to speak we had dinner at my home, and during the meal Norman was the first one that planted that idea in our heads. He told me at that meeting, "What you need here is a union." In other words, the Socialist Party wasn't going to be any help to these tenant farmers. This was after we had taken him out and shown him the conditions in the country and all. And that is where the idea originated, when Thomas told us that. So, after he left, we talked the thing over. Mitchell was actually the big planner in this deal. There was Mitch and myself and two other guys, I think probably Ward Rogers and possibly Alvin Nunnally.

I can't remember just how many there was at the first meeting, but as I remember, it was about fifty-fifty, about half white and half black. We had to have an understanding among the union members, and you couldn't have much understanding if you had two separate unions. So we didn't have any complications to amount to anything about that. I got up and I was pretty hot by that time, and it was, as I said, getting up pretty late and I told them we'd come down here to decide what or whether we was going to have a union or not, and if we was going to have one, well, let's make up our mind and get some members in here. So I took in the first members. They started signing some cards, we had some cards and all there, and these guys joined up.

J.R. Butler: . . . After I had gone back to my sawmill job I got a call from Mitchell, and he told me that they were ready to start building a union there. In fact, I think they had already had a meeting at which they sort of got together on some ideas. So I went back over again, and we worked out a constitution and started organizing. It wasn't long before we had an organizer or two in jail because the plantation element in that part of the country absolutely did not want them "niggers" organized, and they didn't hesitate to say it in just those words. The whites were niggers, too. There was no difference, and some of 'em was beginning to see that there was no difference. Of course, there was still a lot of prejudice among white people in those days, but hard times makes peculiar bedfellows sometimes, and so some of them were beginning to get their eyes open and see that all of them were being used. So it was easy to get a start on organizing.

None of us who were really interested in getting the work started would agree to having a separate union or separate meetings or anything of that kind. A lot of the Negro people agreed with us because they knew that if they had a meeting with just black people there, they wouldn't have any protection whatever, but a few white people might have protective influence, so it was to their interest really to have all of it together.

Of course we had opposition on every hand, the law enforcement officers and the plantation owners and a lot, even, of the white sharecroppers themselves were opposed to an organization that took in both races. But we overcame all of that to some extent and we were ready. As soon as we began to tell people what the situation was and what might be done about it, well, they could see that the white people were being treated just the same as the Negroes, they were in the same boat and they all had to pull together. That's about the best way that I know to express it.

George Stith: . . . When we first started there was no integrated local. Even though white and black organized together, it was set up on the basis of race. It was a community thing. Natu-

rally the communities were segregated. That's why we had segregated locals, because whites and blacks usually didn't live on the farm together. Let me tell you this. When I went to Louisiana in 1953 down in the sugarcane fields, we had the same situation there. Certain plantations were all black and certain plantations were all white. The first time I went to a place called Raceland to make a talk to a group of sugarcane workers, I was the first Negro, except the janitor, that had his foot in the American Legion Hall. The workers were all white, and I went in there that night, and they looked at me sort of funny and said, "Is this who gon' talk?"

Later when we had our district meeting to bring our locals from the whole sugarcane area together, you had the whites and the blacks. And when they sat down and talked and thought of the situation, they decided we were all in the same boat. So they said, "Well, when are y'all gonna meet, we want to come over. When we're gonna meet, we want y'all to come over." This was a thing that just happened. They couldn't see segregation.

Usually we held it in a church or a country schoolhouse. A lot of time they were held without authority, but we could always get in. But the whites had a problem. Where they belonged to a church, the higher-ups also belonged, and they couldn't get the church to have a meeting. So they had to come to a Negro place in order to have a meeting.

Mitchell: Evictions occurred continuously. We estimate something like a half a million or a million as a result of the cotton plow-up program. Dr. Calvin Hoover, who was doing a survey with Howard Odum, estimated a little higher—900,000 evicted as a result of the cotton plow-up in 1933 and the reduction in the cotton program in 1934.

In the beginning, if a union family was evicted and the family wanted to, we'd put them back in the houses. This was done now and then. Usually the plantation owner didn't want them and most of them didn't want to stay. We did that continuously in 1935 because there just wasn't any place for them to go and many people had come back from the city. The relation between the farms and the cities wasn't as close as it is today.

In the beginning, we were trying to get a section of the law enforced providing that sharecroppers should not be evicted from the land because of the operation of this AAA [Agricultural Adjustment Administration] program. We were trying to get that enforced, but of course they didn't pay any attention to the law, any more than they do now when poor people are concerned. We filed a lawsuit in the courts, and about the time the lawsuit was being thrown out, we sent a delegation to Washington to see the secretary of agriculture, Mr. Henry Wallace, the great liberal. As we always did, we had representation of both whites and blacks; there were two other whites besides me and two blacks [Reverend E.B.] McKinney [vice-president of the STFU] and another minister, Reverend N.W. Webb, a union organizer from Birdsong, Arkansas.

We got up early in the morning. Because of the interracial composition of our group, we drove day and night, as there was no place for us to stop and we didn't know what else to do.

Soon after nine o'clock we went back to the Department of Agriculture. We marched up the stairs, the guard had told us the secretary's office was 204. We went right into the secretary's office, and the receptionist asked who we were and we told her we were a delegation from the Southern Tenant Farmers' Union and we wanted to see the secretary. She asked if we had an appointment. Of course we did not. I never heard of having to make an appointment to "see" anybody before. I hesitated and didn't know what to say. McKinney stepped up and said, "Ma'am, we will just sit down here. If Mr. Wallace is busy, we'll just wait until he gets through and we can talk to him then." The receptionist didn't know what to do with a group of people who intended to sit in the office and wait for Mr. Wallace. About that time I remembered a letter I had, addressed to Paul Appleby, the undersecretary of agriculture, and I asked her if she would deliver the letter to Mr. Appleby. Paul Appleby came out and soon he got Henry Wallace out there to see us.

Wallace promised to send an investigator down to investigate the displacement of people under the AAA. We evidently put up a rather convincing story to him.

Stith: . . . They tried to separate people by class, and they tried to do it by race. Whichever was best to use, they used it. It worked on a lot of people, and some people it just didn't work on. For instance, the agent on the plantation where I lived wanted to join the union because he knew the problem, but he was afraid to. And he says to me, "Now George, look, I know you. Anything y'all need that I can give you, just tell me. Information or anything else, I'd get it." . . .

At that time we had a family membership. Where there was a widow involved, she was the head of the family, so she took out a legal membership. But where there was a man and his wife involved, she was a member too. She had a voice when it come down to talking or voting on.

Women were very active and made a lot of the decisions. Women decided to do things that men felt like they couldn't do. We had several locals around Cotton Plant and I believe in one of the locals all the officers were women. This was because men were afraid. Owners never bothered women. They never beat up any women. Oh yes, I think they did in Mississippi and maybe one place in Arkansas. But usually they would pick on the men. They was a little bit slow about bothering women.

Yes, we had some women, and especially there was one that could make just about as good a speech as any of the men could. Henrietta McGee was her name. She went with us on trips to New York and Washington and made speeches before groups and was a big help in getting contributions, because she got right down to earth with the things that she had to say. . . .

Mitchell: There was a kind of unofficial bargaining. They wouldn't recognize the union as such, but they'd watch to see what the union was going to demand, particularly after that cotton picking experience of 1935. We'd call a wage conference every year, maybe twice a year, with several representatives from each local union, and they would decide what we were going to ask for. Often, we'd make a survey of our members and have a ballot to see what they thought the union should ask. We'd do this before the wage conference. Then we'd tabulate all of the returns and say, here's what the members think that we can get. The conference would determine we can get a dollar per hundred this time, and we would announce that the union was demanding a dollar per hundred pounds for picking the cotton. We'd invite all plantation owners to meet with us to work out a contract and an agreement, but of course they never did. This had the same general effect as a wage contract. It was kind of the old IWW idea. If you didn't have a contract, then you take action on the job. If the boss didn't pay the union rate, the people quit work and went somewhere else—where the union scale was paid. . . .

Stith: The problem was that blacks in the agriculture field didn't have leaders with enough education to do what was necessary. That's number one. And number two, a black man wasn't recognized enough to get into the places where he needed to go, even if he had enough education. Even at that time, government organizations didn't look at a black man too much. So a black person as president could not have been too successful in getting a lot of outside help. It was the major role of the union to bring in outside support, money, etc. It had to be. It was the only way we could survive. We had no funds. The members didn't have enough mon-

ey to pay dues to the organization for it to operate. We had to have outside help. A black man was discussed sometimes as being president. And I was discussed at one time. But we decided, that if a black man got to be president it might divide us. So we decided, well at least we'll put him in second spot, make him vice-president.

This is the way most blacks wanted it. There were some few who felt like they were able to lead. When one was found, and he felt thataway, we always found somewhere to put him in a leadership position. I didn't feel like I was a leader. I just wanted to help get things better. But they felt like I was, and they put me into it. . . .

Unfortunately, most of the people coming along now don't know anything about the Southern Tenant Farmers' Union. All the things that the union fought for, that the people on the farms have been able to get, like social security and minimum wage, they just see that the government just give them that. And when you tell them this is something that we fought for for years, that we went to Congress hoboing our way or going in trucks or buses or cars, they don't believe it.

Butler: Most of the unions have gotten to where they're not rank and file anyway. Even the industrial unions are controlled by officials that are elected once every two years or once every four years or sometimes maybe not that often. Back in the earlier days, when people thought about joining the union, it was something like joining a church, getting together to work together for the things they wanted. It was never a mass movement, you know, but it was big enough and so much out of the ordinary that it drew the attention of the world, and so in that way I think we did a lot of good. There were probably things that we could have done if we had known more about what to do, but we were just novices, we just had to play it by ear as we went, and that was all we could do.

Excerpted from Leah Wise and Sue Thrasher, "The Southern Tenant Farmers' Union," in *Working Lives: The Southern Exposure History of Labor in the South,* edited by Marc S. Miller. Reprinted by permission of Southern Exposure.

STUDENT HANDOUT #12-C

"WHY I QUIT THE KLAN"
An Interview with C.P. Ellis

C.P. Ellis was born in 1927 and was fifty-three years old at the time of this interview with Studs Terkel. At one time he was president (Exalted Cyclops) of the Durham chapter of the Ku Klux Klan, and lived in Durham, North Carolina.

All my life, I had work, never a day without work, worked all the overtime I could get and still could not survive financially. I began to see there's something wrong with this country. I worked my butt off and just never seemed to break even. I had some real great ideas about this nation. They say to abide by the law, go to church, do right and live for the Lord, and everything'll work out. But it didn't work out. It just kept getting worse and worse. . . .

Tryin to come out of that hole, I just couldn't do it. I really began to get bitter. I didn't know who to blame. I tried to find somebody. Hatin America is hard to do because you can't see it to hate it. You gotta have somethin to look at to hate. The natural person for me to hate would be black people, because my father before me was a member of the Klan. . . .

So I began to admire the Klan. . . . To be part of somethin. . . . The first night I went with the fellas . . . I was led into a large meeting room, and this was the time of my life! It was thrilling. Here's a guy who's worked all his life and struggled all his life to be something, and here's the moment to be something. I will never forget it. Four robed Klansmen led me into the hall. The lights were dim and the only thing you could see was an illuminated cross. . . . After I had taken my oath, there was loud applause goin throughout the buildin, musta been at least four hundred people. For this one little ol person. It was a thrilling moment for C.P. Ellis. . . .

The majority of [the Klansmen] are low-income whites, people who really don't have a part in something. They have been shut out as well as blacks. Some are not very well educated either. Just like myself. We had a lot of support from doctors and lawyers and police officers.

Maybe they've had bitter experiences in this life and they had to hate somebody. So the natural person to hate would be the black person. He's beginnin to come up, he's beginnin to . . . start votin and run for political office. Here are white people who are supposed to be superior to them, and we're shut out. . . . Shut out. Deep down inside, we want to be part of this great society. Nobody listens, so we join these groups. . . .

We would go to the city council meetings and the blacks would be there and we'd be there. It was a confrontation every time. . . . We began to make some inroads with the city councilmen and county commissioners. They began to call us friend. Call us at night on the telephone: "C.P., glad you came to that meeting last night." They didn't want integration either, but they did it secretively, in order to get elected. They couldn't stand up openly and say it, but they were glad somebody was sayin it. We visited some of the city leaders in their homes and talked to em privately. It wasn't long before councilmen would call me up: "The blacks are comin up tonight and makin outrageous demands. How about some of you people showin up and have a little balance?". . . .

We'd load up our cars and we'd fill up half the council chambers, and the blacks the other half. During these times, I carried weapons to the meetings, outside my belt. We'd go there armed. We would wind up just hollerin and fussin at each other. What happened? As a result of our fightin one another, the city council still had their way. They didn't want to give up control to the blacks nor the Klan. They were usin us.

I began to realize this later down the road. One day I was walkin downtown and a certain city council member saw me comin. I expected him to shake my hand because he was talkin to me at night on the telephone. I had been in his home and visited with him. He crossed the street [to avoid me]. . . . I began to think, somethin's wrong here. Most of em are merchants or maybe an attorney, an insurance agent, people like that. As long as they kept low-income whites and low-income blacks fightin, they're gonna maintain control. I began to get that feelin after I was ignored in public. I thought: . . . you're not gonna use me any more. That's when I began to do some real serious thinkin.

The same thing is happening in this country today. People are being used by those in control, those who have all the wealth. I'm not espousing communism. We got the greatest system of government in the world. But those who have it simply don't want those who don't have it to have any part of it. Black and white. When it comes to money, the green, the other colors make no difference.

I spent a lot of sleepless nights. I still didn't like blacks. I didn't want to associate with them. Blacks, Jews, or Catholics. My father said: "Don't have anything to do with em." I didn't until I met a black person and talked with him, eyeball to eyeball, and met a Jewish person and talked to him, eyeball to eyeball. I found they're people just like me. They cried, they cussed, they prayed, they had desires. Just like myself. Thank God, I got to the point where I can look past labels. But at that time, my mind was closed.

I remember one Monday night Klan meeting. I said something was wrong. Our city fathers were using us. And I didn't like to be used. The reactions of the others was not too pleasant: "Let's just keep fightin them niggers."

I'd go home at night and I'd have to wrestle with myself. I'd look at a black person walkin down the street, and the guy'd have ragged shoes or his clothes would be worn. That began to do something to me inside. I went through this for about six months. I felt I just had to get

out of the Klan. But I wouldn't get out. . . .

[Ellis was invited, as a Klansman, to join a committee of people from all walks of life to make recommendations on how to solve racial problems in the school system. He very reluctantly accepted. After a few stormy meetings, he was elected co-chair of the committee, along with Ann Atwater, a black woman who for years had been leading local efforts for civil rights.]

A Klansman and a militant black woman, co-chairmen of the school committee. It was impossible. How could I work with her? But it was in our hands. We had to make it a success. This gave me another sense of belongin, a sense of pride. This helped the inferiority feeling I had. A man who has stood up publicly and said he despised black people, all of a sudden he was willin to work with em. Here's a chance for a low-income white man to be somethin. In spite of all my hatred for blacks and Jews and liberals, I accepted the job. Her and I began to reluctantly work together. She had as many problems workin with me as I had workin with her.

One night, I called her: "Ann, you and I should have a lot of differences and we got em now. But there's somethin laid out here before us, and if it's gonna be a success, you and I are gonna have to make it one. Can we lay aside some of these feelins?" She said: "I'm willing if you are." I said: "Let's do it."

My old friends would call me at night: "C.P., what the hell is wrong with you? You're sellin out the white race." This begin to make me have guilt feelins. Am I doin right? Am I doin wrong? Here I am all of a sudden makin an about-face and tryin to deal with my feelins, my heart. My mind was beginnin to open up. I was beginnin to see what was right and what was wrong. I don't want the kids to fight forever. . . .

One day, Ann and I went back to the school and we sat down. We began to talk and just reflect. . . . I begin to see, here we are, two people from the far ends of the fence, havin identical problems, except hers bein black and me bein white. . . . The amazing thing about it, her and I, up to that point, has cussed each other, bawled each other, we hated each other. Up to that point, we didn't know each other. We didn't know we had things in common. . . .

The whole world was openin up, and I was

learning new truths that I had never learned before. I was beginning to look at a black person, shake hands with him, and see him as a human bein. I hadn't got rid of all this stuff. I've still got a little bit of it. But somethin was happenin to me. . . .

I come to work one morning and some guys says: "We need a union." At this time I wasn't pro-union. My daddy was antilabor too. We're not gettin paid much, we're havin to work seven days in a row. We're all starvin to death. . . . I didn't know nothin about organizin unions, but I knew how to organize people, stir people up. That's how I got to be business agent for the union.

When I began to organize, I began to see far deeper. I begin to see people again bein used. Blacks against whites. . . . There are two things management wants to keep: all the money and all the say-so. They don't want none of these poor workin folks to have none of that. I begin to see management fightin me with everythin they had. Hire antiunion law firms, badmouth unions. The people were makin $1.95 an hour, barely able to get through weekends. . . .

It makes you feel good to go into a plant and . . . see black people and white people join hands and defeat the racist issues [union-busters] use against people. . . .

I tell people there's a tremendous possibility in this country to stop wars, the battles, the struggles, the fights between people. People say: "That's an impossible dream. You sound like Martin Luther King." An ex-Klansman who sounds like Martin Luther King. I don't think it's an impossible dream. It's happened in my life. It's happened in other people's lives in America. . . .

When the news came over the radio that Martin Luther King was assassinated, I got on the telephone and begin to call other Klansmen. . . .

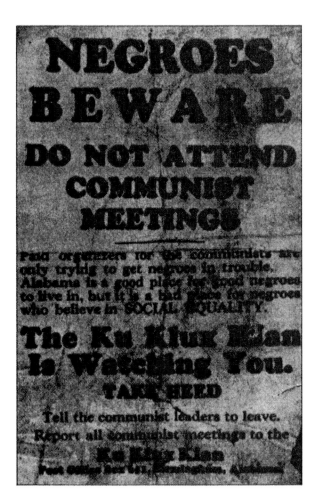

We just had a real party. . . . Really rejoicin cause the son of a bitch was dead. Our troubles are over with. They say the older you get, the harder it is for you to change. That's not necessarily true. Since I changed, I've set down and listened to tapes of Martin Luther King. I listen to it and tears come to my eyes cause I know what he's sayin now. I know what's happenin.

From Studs Terkel, *American Dreams: Lost and Found*, copyright © 1980 by Studs Terkel. Reprinted by permission of Pantheon Books, a division of Random House, Inc.

STUDENT HANDOUT #13-A

TERMS YOU SHOULD KNOW

Longshoremen: The people who work on the docks loading and unloading the ships.

Gang boss or foreman: The person who is directly in charge of the longshoremen. Before the strike the gang boss would hire the longshoremen and tell them how long to work. This boss was hired by the Waterfront Employers' Association.

International Longshoremen's Association: The union of longshoremen in 1934.

Stevedore company: Shipping companies hire stevedore companies—also known as Waterfront Employers—to load and unload cargo on their ships. These stevedore companies then hire gang bosses who hire longshoremen.

Waterfront Employers' Association: The organization of all the stevedore companies in Portland.

Union recognition: When employers agree to negotiate wages, hours, and working conditions *only* with the union instead of with separate individuals.

Picket line: A group of workers gathered at the company(ies) they are striking against. Sometimes these workers try physically to stop people from entering the workplace. Other times they picket to show that they are on strike and to convince people to support them and not to go to work.

Scab: A name people on strike call a person who crosses a picket line to work at a job a striker usually does.

Hiring hall: The place where longshoremen wait to be hired.

STUDENT HANDOUT #13-B

PORTLAND DAILY NEWS
May 9, 1934

Longshoremen Out on Strike!!

Tomorrow morning has been set by longshoremen as the beginning of their coastwide strike. We have asked the International Longshoremen's Association (ILA) and the Waterfront Employers' Association (WEA) to present their differing points of view to the public. The following are editorials representing these views.

Terrible Conditions Force Strike by the ILA

Longshoremen on the West Coast have taken enough! For years the employers have pushed us around like we were their little play things. We are on strike to win better conditions and to regain our dignity.

Ever since the Depression hit Portland—back in early 1930—the employers have been squeezing us to death. Often employers force longshoremen to work double shifts—sometimes even as long as thirty-six hours without sleep! This makes work very unsafe. Many workers have been killed or badly injured due to carelessness caused by lack of sleep. Some longshoremen are forced to work eighty hours a week while others work as few as eight. And, of course, many are *totally* without work.

To get a job has become a humiliation. The employers hire "gang bosses" who demand bribes of bottles of whiskey or money. The bosses want only the biggest and strongest men, so older workers are often without work. They also try to hire men not in the union.

The Depression has given employers an excuse to cut our pay. They slashed it from $.90 an hour down to $.75. But when they saw the union was gaining strength they raised wages to $.85—and tried to make it look like they were doing us a favor.

While they're busy cutting our wages, employers are also speeding up the work. Many gangs have been forced to handle over three times as much cargo as they were just a few years ago!

The employers have left us no choice. They are causing us to strike.

Our demands are simple:

(1) The employers must recognize our union—the ILA. They must agree to bargain ("negotiate") with the union in every port on the West Coast—and *only* with the union. (The phony Columbia River Longshoremen's Association was created by the employers to slow our organizing—it hasn't worked.) No more playing one man off against another. Our slogan is, "An injury to one is an injury to all."

(2) We want a "union-controlled hiring hall." In other words, the union should decide who would be hired to work on the longshore. We want to rotate jobs among *all* longshoremen so that everyone works about the same: No one works too much or too little. No more having to bribe gang bosses!

(3) We demand a six-hour day and a thirty-hour week. A shorter work day will lead to fewer injuries. Also, it will mean more work to be shared with many of the unemployed workers.

(4) We want an increase in pay from $.85 an hour to $1.00 an hour and for overtime from $1.25 an hour to $1.50. This is a decent living wage.

The employers have started this strike—but we'll finish it. We urge Oregonians to support the longshoremen.

Selfish Longshoremen Unreasonable, Greedy by the WEA

Some longshoremen are going on strike. Thinking only of themselves, they will be hurting everyone in the entire state of Oregon.

The Waterfront Employers have done everything we can to avoid this strike. Longshoremen claim that conditions are getting worse. Actually they're getting better. Last year employers increased wages from $.75 to $.85 an hour. This is a generous offer, made at a time when many of us are losing money.

Just looking at the longshoremen's demands, we can see what an irresponsible strike this is. They want the *union* to control hiring! Please, name one single industry where workers get to hire workers. This is a ridiculous demand, just on the face of it.

They want us to recognize the union. We are not opposed to unions. But longshoremen in Portland already have a union. It's called the Columbia River Longshoremen's Association. We are fully supportive of them. In fact, we even helped get this union started.

Longshoremen demand a six-hour day. This is silly. Even *they* must realize this. Whoever heard of a six-hour workday? We suspect some good old-fashioned laziness is at the root of this demand.

And finally, their demand for increased wages. They must think we're made of money. Having increased wages $.10 an hour last year, they now whine for a $.15 increase on top of that. If this doesn't show their greed, then what does?

We are in a Depression. Everyone is hurting. Our profits have suffered enormously. But we're not complaining—we realize that all Oregonians are in this thing together. However, we do feel that the longshoremen should not try to force us out of business with their selfish demands.

Longshoremen have threatened to use violence to keep the docks closed. This is regrettable. The WEA believes that in a civilized society disputes should be handled calmly and reasonably. However, should the longshoremen carry through with their threat of violence, we know the police will protect our property rights.

We also know that there are many people out there wanting work. We urge unemployed people to come forward and take the jobs of these strikers who have such little concern for the people of Oregon. We are counting on your support.

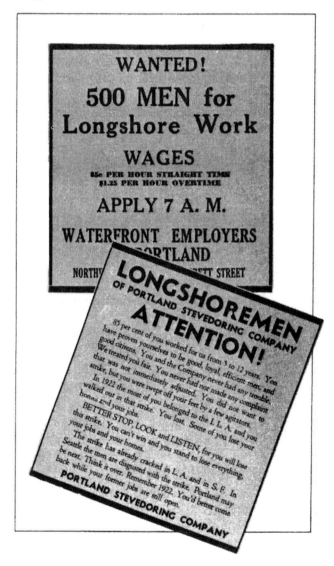

STUDENT HANDOUT #13-C

LONGSHOREMAN

Before the strike you had been working on the docks in a "steel gang" (a group of workers who mostly load and unload steel from the ships). There has been less and less work for longshoremen since about 1930. The way the Waterfront Employers hire people has made it impossible to feel secure about getting enough money each week to live on. You have to be down at the hiring hall all day long whether or not there's any work.

Sometimes you go home, having spent all day on the longshore without any wages for your wasted time. When there *is* work, a "gang boss," hired by one of the Waterfront Employers, will go around picking men he wants in his gang. Often he chooses people who give him bribes of whiskey or money, but because you're very strong and a good worker you haven't had to offer any bribes . . . yet. You're thirty-two years old and all the time there are more and more younger people coming along who are eager for your job.

Often, the Waterfront Employers say that because there won't be much work the next day they'll only hire the gangs which work the fastest today. This means that your gang boss will make you work fast and very, very hard to compete with the other gangs. Some days you work as many as *thirty-six hours straight,*

stopping only for short breaks. There are times when you work close to eighty hours in a week, rarely seeing your family. Other weeks you might get five to ten hours work (or none at all) and have trouble paying your family's bills.

Another thing the Waterfront Employers have done during the past few years has been to cut your wages. In 1930, you were getting $.90 an hour. In 1933 they cut wages to $.75 an hour. It's only because they're scared of the union that they recently boosted wages back to $.85 an hour.

Last year because of the speed-ups in your work, a good friend of yours lost one of his hands in an accident. You had been working for twenty-four hours straight, with only two short breaks. The accident happened because your friend wasn't awake enough to pay attention and his hand got caught between thick steel rods.

With the strike now on, you'll need to get support from as many groups as possible. The strike could hurt some groups—especially farmers who depend on shipping to sell their produce and to obtain fertilizers, baling wire, gasoline, etc.

You'll need to think of ways to get these farmers—and others—on your side.

STUDENT HANDOUT #13-D

UNEMPLOYED PERSON

You've been looking for a job for over a year, but you just can't find anything at all. You're beginning to wonder if there's something wrong with *you*. You have relatives in town who help out some, and you have a vegetable garden, but you're worried about your family's health. You are married and have two kids.

You've stopped paying rent on your house because you can't afford it. Your landlady has threatened to kick you out if you don't pay up. You don't know whether or not to believe her. Some empty houses have been torn apart for wood to burn for heat. She might be worried the same thing could happen to her house if she kicks you out. But you can't be too sure.

What you'd really like is a steady job that pays well so that you can feed and clothe your family and feel better about your own self-worth. You couldn't even afford to buy anything for your kids for Christmas. You're feeling more desperate all the time.

You have many skills and could work at any number of jobs. You've been a carpenter, you know how to lay bricks, you've worked in the lumber mills for a time, and even spent a year working as a longshoreman.

Recently, you have joined one of Portland's unemployed councils. This is kind of like a union of unemployed people. These councils work to keep people's water, gas, and electricity turned on, even when they can't pay their bills. Sometimes if the city turns off a family's water someone from the council will come over and turn it back on.

The councils believe that unemployed people have to stick together with working people and to support each other. Council leaders talk a lot about people who aren't owners or bosses needing to help each other fight to get what they need.

STUDENT HANDOUT #13-E

WATERFRONT EMPLOYER

Steamship companies hire your company to load and unload their ships. In turn, you hire longshoremen to actually do the work. The Depression has been making your life difficult.

First, because of the Depression there isn't as much shipping going on. So all the Waterfront Employers have been busy competing with each other trying to offer a lower price to the steamship companies, hoping to get more business for *themselves*. This means that your profits have been lower than before.

Also, you still owe the bank a large part of the money you borrowed early in 1929 to expand your operations on the waterfront. You had hoped for more business but you've gotten less. Each month you need to make large payments on the money you borrowed, and you're worried you might not be able to keep them up. And, of course, now you've got the longshoremen, the people who actually do the work of loading and unloading ships, making new demands on you.

Ever since 1922 you haven't had to deal with any longshoremen unions. You have been able to hire and fire anyone you wanted. You could pretty much decide how many hours at a time people would work. Since 1930 you've been able to lower wages and still find people willing to work. All the major decisions have been up to the small group of men who sit with you on the board of directors of the Portland Stevedoring Company, and you've gotten used to that.

You are a very important person. You can't understand why you should share your power with a bunch of uneducated longshoremen.

It's lucky for you that all the Waterfront Employers have their own "union," the Waterfront Employers' Association, where they can make plans during the strike.

Many businesses in the area use the port either to ship their goods or to get supplies. Everyone's gasoline is brought in by ship and many items sold by stores around Portland are shipped in from around the world and from other U.S. ports. The lumber mills use the port to ship their products out to the rest of the world. Farmers also use the port to ship many of their products to other cities and other countries. You can see how important your business is to the whole area around Portland.

STUDENT HANDOUT #13-F

FARMER

You own a small farm in the Tualatin Valley outside of Portland. You grow things like wheat and some vegetables. Since the Depression started, you've barely been making enough money from the sales of your produce to feed and clothe your family and pay expenses. You have a small amount of savings, but nothing substantial. A year when sales fall off could force you to borrow from the bank in order to get the seed and supplies to plant for the next year.

You sell most of your wheat to grain wholesalers in Portland who sometimes ship your produce outside the state by water. The vegetables you sell end up mostly in the small groceries around the Portland area. The wholesalers tend to have quite a bit of control over the price you get for your produce. You're not very fond of these people, whom you consider the "big guys."

So far this spring has been a good growing season. If all goes well, this might be a prosperous year for you and your family. You'll certainly need your farm equipment in good shape. You buy the oil and gas for your tractor in Portland; it comes to the port of Portland on tanker ships. Other necessities you use, like baling wire, also arrive by ship.

A major fear you have is that you could lose everything. Some families you know have just given up trying to farm and have moved to Portland. They get whatever jobs they can: as mill workers, clerks, railroad workers, longshoremen. Some people can't find jobs at all. Those who can are often treated poorly—they have dangerous working conditions and get low wages. You are sympathetic to their problems; the Depression has been tough on everyone, and people need to help each other out in these hard times.

The strike puts you in a rough spot. You certainly have no love for the Waterfront Employers or the shipping companies—often the same people. The way you look at it, it's been their high prices that have helped keep you poor. You're not anxious for these people to become any *more* powerful.

But if you can't ship your wheat or buy needed supplies, you could go broke.

STUDENT HANDOUT #13-G

CENTRAL LABOR COUNCIL REPRESENTATIVE

You're a carpenter and you're in the carpenters' union in Portland. You also hold a very interesting and important position during the longshore strike. You are a member of the Strike Investigation Committee of the Central Labor Council.

The Central Labor Council is like the coordinating committee of all the unions in Portland. It is a very important organization, combining unions with a total membership of *20,000 workers*.

The council has assigned you as representative to look into the longshore strike and to help figure out whether to support the strike and if so *how* to support it.

You will have to examine closely the issues involved because you know that not all union people in Portland feel the same about the strike.

For example, because the strike has shut down the port of Portland, many workers have been laid off. No shipping means less trucking, less repair work, etc. A long strike could mean serious hardships for those workers and their families. So, many union people in Portland would like to see the strike come to a quick end.

However, union people realize that if the longshoremen lose the strike, their wages will stay low, their hours long, and their employers will be even more powerful. This could encourage other employers in Portland to try to get rid of the unions they negotiate with. At the very least, other employers might try to cut wages and lengthen hours. If the longshoremen lose, workers all over the city might feel demoralized and beaten down.

At this point, you feel pulled in both directions: (1) You want a quick end to the strike, but (2) you worry about what would happen if the longshoremen were to lose.

STUDENT HANDOUT #13-H

QUESTIONS FACING YOUR GROUP

1. Do you support the longshoremen's strike? Why or why not?

2. What is your proposal for how the strike could be settled?

3. Should Governor Meier order the Oregon National Guard into Portland to protect workers who are willing to cross the longshoremen's picket line and break the strike? Explain.

4. What action will your group take if Meier *does* order the Guard in? What action will you take if he doesn't?

STUDENT HANDOUT #13-I

LONGSHORE ROLE PLAY
Summing Up

1. Who or what could be blamed for the longshore strike?

2. Explain the position your group took on the strike and why you decided on that position.

3. What kind of power did your social group have? Where did your power come from?

4. How did you feel about Governor Meier's decision not to call the Oregon National Guard into Portland?

BACKGROUND NOTES
AGITATE, EDUCATE, ORGANIZE: PORTLAND, 1934

It was known as the "Big Strike"—the 1934 longshore strike. For over two months the walkout paralyzed shipping from California to Washington; its organization and objectives inspired workers across the country.

The action was called by the West Coast District of the International Longshoremen's Association (ILA). And though just one strike, it was characterized by different tactics and consequences in each of the idled ports. In Portland, Oregon, events unfolded in ways that would affirm valuable lessons for the labor movement throughout the entire country.

Conditions on the Portland waterfront in 1934 were summed up by Ernie Baker, a longshoreman active in the strike: "Absolutely, downright miserable"—and getting worse. Throughout the 1920s, the security of the longshoremen's jobs rested on the whims of the foremen, known as "gang bosses." Union members (whether ILA or Industrial Workers of the World—IWW) were blacklisted when discovered. Jobs could be had by "cooperative" workers. Matt Meehan, an ILA organizer, remembered what some people were forced to endure:

"A man had to pay for his job, kick back, and oh yes, the gang boss would always leave about three jobs open on his pad so he could take care of his friends, relatives, what have you. The dispatchers had favorites too. [Longshoremen] were kicking in to the people who were running the hiring hall—if not in cash, they would bring them little presents like a fifth. A lot of times people would give the dispatchers ham or something. That was the kind of thing that was going on on the waterfront."

The Depression set in motion a chain of events that put new strains on those longshoremen lucky enough to have jobs. With stevedore companies competing fiercely to obtain the scarcer business of shipping companies, gang bosses were ordered to speed up the work to unheard-of levels. Lumber gangs, used to handling 25,000 board feet a day, were pushed to

the frantic pace of 65,000 to 85,000 feet. There was no improvement of equipment: just harder, longer work. Shifts of fifteen hours were common; thirty-six became increasingly frequent.

Gangs pliant enough to go along with this speed were rewarded with regular work. Other gangs, however, worked as little as eight to ten hours a week.

For awhile, scarcity of work forced most people to put up with these conditions. Matt Meehan was probably only half joking when he cracked: "The competition for jobs was such, well, like honest-to-Christ, as a young married man some nights I couldn't do my homework. It was that bad."

Frequent injuries were the result of the longer work days—though often longshoremen would be afraid to report them. In the fear-ridden climate of the pre-strike years, workers worried that an injury report could get them fired.

The docks had always been a place unemployed workers might hope to secure a job. Those now out of work, their numbers swollen by the Depression, headed for the docks. Stevedore companies took advantage of this surplus of workers to cut wages. Pay for longshoremen dropped from $.90 an hour in 1930 to $.75 in 1933. Worried by the ILA's growing popularity and the potential for a strike, wages were boosted to $.85 in early 1934.

The organizers of the local ILA had learned from their own past failures. Matt Meehan's experiences are illustrative. Meehan began his maritime career as a seaman. The first strike he joined, "We were out there on the picket line and the longshoremen would walk right through and they'd wave to us, 'Hi, fellas.'" It became clear to Meehan and others that success could only come from industrywide solidarity. Workers in and around the port, though they might be in different unions, would have to support each other's strikes.

The loss of the 1922 longshore strike served

Meehan as a university course in what *not* to do in a strike. "You see, the ports went out individually, and since the strike had gotten no support from the International, financial or otherwise, the employers were able to beat the ports one at a time." Meehan says the ILA had wisely concluded by 1934 that "when one local strikes, all the locals strike, and we have the same demands. We'd go out on the same day, and go back on the same day, all the contracts would be the same."

Strike Goals

The single most important goal of the ILA was union recognition. Without employer recognition of the union as official bargaining agent, workers would be limited in their ability to defend themselves. From November until March 1934 the employers along the coast had steadfastly rejected that single demand. Attempts to talk with the owners had gotten longshoremen nowhere; the leadership of the union proposed a coastwide strike.

Final approval rested with the membership. The strike vote, taken in each port in March, was an overwhelming eleven-to-one margin in favor of a walkout. Its starting date was delayed by a personal plea from President Roosevelt, but May 9, 1934, saw all West Coast ports out on strike.

The first demand, of course, was for union recognition. Just as important to the strikers was the goal of a union-controlled hiring hall. The years of favoritism and bribery for work had convinced longshoremen that the only trustworthy hiring procedure was one run by themselves. Further, they demanded a reduction in "straight" time from eight to six hours, and a thirty-hour week. The intention was to help spread available work—a fact not lost on the many unemployed longshoremen.

Wages, though by no means the major issue in the strike, were also a concern. Longshoremen wanted straight-time pay boosted from $.85 an hour to $1.00, and overtime from $1.25 to $1.50.

The employers rejected all these demands. They called for the open shop (i.e., business as usual), employer-operated hiring halls, port-by-port elections to determine union representation, and bargaining by individual ports.

To the longshoremen, their bosses' offer was a transparent attempt to divide and conquer. They were adamant: Any agreement reached must be voted on by membership in all ports; and no longshoremen would return to work until the other maritime unions, also on strike, had gotten satisfaction on their demands.

The Question of the Unemployed

Their employers were confident of victory, believing that with high unemployment, strikebreakers would be easy to find. E.C. Davis, of the Waterfront Employers' Association in Portland, stated assuredly that the depressed economic situation "created a large supply of men who could be called on to work on the docks if the regularly employed longshoremen refused to work."

Longshoremen, too, realized that if the unemployed crossed their picket lines en masse, their strike would be crushed. They concluded, long before their walkout, that they would seek the support of people out of work.

Beginning in the winter of 1929–30, the Communist Party had organized unemployed councils throughout the country. In Portland, by the spring of 1934 these councils had won much support among the unemployed. Dirk De Jonge, a council organizer, talked about how they worked:

"The Unemployed Council in Portland, for instance, set up sub-organizations in different districts of the city. They elected their own leaders and whatever complaint was presented, they would take action as to what to do. For example, a person comes in there and says his water has been shut off 'cause he couldn't pay his bill. Well, the Unemployed Council in that particular part of the city would simply go and turn on the water. It was the same with natural gas. . . . People wouldn't pay their bills because they didn't have the money anyway. They would take their complaint to the welfare. Each part of the city had their own programs, their own activities."

Months before the strike, the longshoremen sent delegations to the councils explaining the issues and asking for their support. Longshoreman Ernie Baker claimed success. " 'If it's gonna help you, it's gonna help us eventually.' That's the attitude these fellas had." And he concluded: "We got ourselves an ally."

Matt Meehan agreed. "All during the strike there wasn't one of those unemployed groups, not one man, that scabbed. Not one of them broke ranks, not one of them went to work on the waterfront. They were down there—one day there was 5,000 down there on the picket line."

For their part, longshoremen were active helping unemployed workers and their families. Strike commissaries welcomed them, sharing the food that had been donated by farmers and other unions. And longshoremen scoured the city searching for floor space in warehouses to accommodate families without homes.

Strikers relied mainly on this working-class solidarity to keep the docks shut, but they also felt force would need to play a role. Scabbing, as they saw it, was the worst form of theft. A scab stole the jobs men had sweated for their entire working lives—robbing, as well, the future security of their families. The police, enforcing laws set up to protect the employers' control over their private property, did not see a scab as a criminal. Therefore, it would be up to the longshoremen to stop the criminal in the act.

The Strike Begins

On the morning of May 10, the second day of the strike, employers sat in their hiring hall anxiously awaiting men to show up for work. They'd threatened that longshoremen still absent by 8 a.m. would be fired. By 9 o'clock, the hall held just 150 men—mostly gang bosses. Outside, about a thousand strikers surrounding the hall were determined that no cargo would be unloaded on the docks.

Shortly after nine the employers foolishly called for buses to transport the strikebreakers to various worksites. Longshoremen greeted the buses by ordering them to stop and rocking them back and forth until they were almost overturned. The drivers and guards scurried inside to the safety of the hall. Later attempts to move the men to the docks failed. At 3 p.m. police patrol wagons arrived to escort the 150 away.

As a precaution against further strikebreaking activity, longshoremen formed "flying squads." "That's where those old boxers and wrestlers came in handy, those football players," Meehan remembered. "They used to put the fear of God into all the ones who used to try and get in on that job to scab."

The violence of the strikers—in self-defense, as they saw it—certainly helped discourage would-be stevedores. But more important to the outcome of the strike was the ILA's success in getting its members to secure widespread support for their cause.

At least half of the leadership of the strike had earlier been active in the IWW. These men had

a class-conscious sense of "us against them," as well as very definite ideas about how to run a strike. While not rejecting the notion of raising money to support people on strike, they felt that keeping the union's membership involved was more important. People needed to be out talking, recruiting allies and securing supplies. Insuring that strikers stayed active would be the best tonic for low morale. Not only did relying on lots of money fail to win strikes, according to the IWW, but it also helped erode union democracy. "The most conservative unions are always those with the largest treasuries," warned the *Industrial Worker,* the IWW newspaper.

For Wobblies, winning was only one of the goals of a strike; another was educating. A strike showed workers their power to change job conditions—more importantly, it demonstrated that they could transform the entire society. Rank-and-file control, mass involvement, working-class solidarity: the IWW taught that these were characteristics of the new society they were aiming for, as well as winning tactics.

Harvesting Support

The longshoremen knew that the Oregon farmers would need to be convinced that the strike was in their interests; like an army, a strike travels on its stomach. And, in the long run, ILA leaders knew that any social movement for lasting change would need the farmers' participation.

The ILA arranged for speakers to travel throughout the state explaining the strike and soliciting aid. Farmers responded. The United Farmers' League gave its endorsement to the longshoremen and made donations to keep the strike commissary full. According to former longshoreman Jack Mowery, "We had a beautiful set-up with the people around the country here, the farmers, what we called the poor farmers. We got all kinds of donations of vegetables, fruits, and everything else. We sent pickets out to help them gather their crops."

On July 4, twenty-five farmers from the Oregon coast dug clams for the striking long-shoremen. With the clams came their promise of further aid, their prayers for success, and a request for more union speakers. Ernie Baker remembers one farmer who brought a live pig to the commissary. He butchered it, dressed it, and presented it to the strikers.

It was probably more than just kindness that motivated the farmers' generosity toward the strikers. As longshoremen organized, so did farmers. In one nearby county, membership in the National Farmers' Union went from zero to seven hundred in less than two years. Especially angered by the banks and railroads, farmers could see that they shared a common foe with longshoremen: corporate control over decisions affecting their livelihoods.

The ILA, appreciating the support and eager to solidify its budding alliance with the farmers, agreed to release gasoline—provided the farmers actually got it. The union also arranged to pull some of their pickets, so much-needed baling wire and fertilizers could be picked up by the farmers. Longshoremen were even on hand to help the farmers load supplies onto trucks. ILA member Toby Christensen remembers, "Employers couldn't say anything about it. We outnumbered them." Worried about the loss of cannery jobs, the longshoremen also issued permits to release fresh fruit and sugar. In early July, it was reported that the ILA had offered to negotiate the loading of Oregon's wheat crop. The shippers refused to discuss whether or not the cargo should be handled.

While most farmers apparently were sympathetic toward the strike, according to one report some farm co-ops telegrammed Governor Meier, urging him to call out the National Guard to end the walkout. (In a later longshore strike, employers bused seed farmers' wives to Portland for a demonstration opposing the strike. Longshoremen's wives met the women on the docks, inviting them to the union hall where refreshments had been prepared. After listening to arguments for the strike, farmers' wives apologized, explaining they'd been misled.)

Longshoremen were especially eager for support in Portland. Ernie Baker worked with the "Propaganda Department": "We fanned out all over the city. We covered it like a blanket." Jack Mowery recalled, "We went to the small grocerymen, neighborhood groceries, and so forth—which was many in those days. . . . We went to the churches, all those places, and set this all up two months ahead of time." The ILA also took to the air waves, broadcasting a nightly fifteen-minute update over a local radio station. Scripts for each program, Baker explained, were tailored to address the concerns longshoremen heard as they canvassed neighborhoods.

Enter the International

Ironically, at a time when so many different groups were offering aid to the strike, longshoremen were fighting the leadership of their own International. On two separate occasions, ILA President Joseph Ryan unilaterally signed agreements with employers, ostensibly ending the strike.

Because of the ILA structure, with its relatively autonomous districts, Ryan had only limited authority in the West. In his home base of New York City, his control rested on dispensing patronage to favored members and on the close relations he maintained with employers. There, he was able to keep union dissidents from being hired on the waterfront and, when sufficient pressure grew from below, to come up with a raise for his members.

Rank-and-file militancy threatened the control he hoped to extend nationally. On his arrival in the West he declared, "We don't give a hoot for the closed shop. All we are interested in is recognition with preference." In fact, a union-controlled hiring hall—essentially a closed shop—was precisely what the strike was all about.

Ryan's first agreement so disgusted Portland longshoremen that they wouldn't even take ballots. Undaunted, Ryan on June 16 signed a second agreement. He exclaimed exuberantly, "There is no question but that they [the members] will approve and ratify it." The agreement, which still included no provision for a union-controlled hiring hall, was voted down in every port except San Pedro. The ILA president, having flunked his course in union democracy, gave up and returned to New York.

Violence in San Francisco

With Ryan's acquiescent voice silenced and the strikers holding firm, no settlement appeared possible. Employers in San Francisco decided it was time to break the strike. On July 3, five truckloads of men, protected by seven hundred police, cruised slowly from the pier toward the warehouses. A police captain yelled, "The port is open!" The cry sparked a battle between thousands of strikers and their supporters and the police. Twenty-five people were hospitalized.

Two days later five thousand people clashed with police. In what became known as "Bloody Thursday," hundreds of people were injured and three were killed. The next day California Governor Merriam dispatched the National Guard. Organized labor in San Francisco responded by calling a general strike: 130,000 workers walked off their jobs.

The battles in San Francisco put Portland longshoremen on alert. As early as the third day of the strike, Mayor Joseph Carson pleaded with Governor Meier to send in the National Guard and open the port. The Central Labor Council then threatened that if the Guard were used in Portland, there would be a general strike. Meier refused to act on Carson's request.

On the Fourth of July, fifty-four picketers were arrested by police near some oil docks. On July 6, eighty Portland unions met to form a general strike committee. The announcement was made that a general strike vote would be held following any violence initiated by the employers or police.

Meier sent a frantic message to President Roosevelt: "We are now in a state of armed hostilities." He pleaded with the President to act immediately "to prevent insurrection which, if not checked, will develop into civil war." Rejected by FDR, the governor mobilized the Guard and encamped them near Portland; however, he did not actually send them into the "hostilities."

Matt Meehan speculated that the longshoremen's picketing of the Meier and Frank department store in downtown Portland helped the governor understand his potential financial losses should he use the Guard. (Julius Meier was a major stockholder in his family's retail store business.) And it was reported that longshoremen's wives, having earlier organized an auxiliary, were sticking customers with hat pins whenever they crossed picket lines.

More likely, Meier had larger concerns. Facing the threat of a general strike, waged on behalf of a cause with widespread support, the governor decided to back off. The Guard would not move to open the port.

The Employers Surrender

Met by one sound defeat after another and confronted by the continuing general strike in San Francisco, employers gave up. They agreed to arbitration by the National Longshoremen's Board, which had been formed earlier by President Roosevelt. Union leaders, who had proposed arbitration back in mid-May, immediately put the employers' offer to a coastwide vote. The overwhelming ILA ratification ended the strike. Pending the arbitration settlement, longshoremen returned to work on July 31, 1934.

In San Francisco, longshore leader Harry Bridges cautioned workers against forgetting the source of their power. "We may receive some betterment of conditions through arbitration, but that may be in the future. So it behooves us to take an aggressive attitude and establish and improve working conditions on our own initiative." (Heeding Bridges' advice, over the next two years West Coast longshoremen "hung the hook"—struck—over five hundred times, acting on their own and others' grievances.)

On October 12, the Longshoremen's Board handed down the final award. Perhaps a result of workers' ongoing militancy, the decision represented a clearcut victory for the union. The ILA was established as the coast-wide bargaining agent for longshoremen. There would be a thirty-hour week and a six-hour day. Straight time would be paid at $.95 an hour, with overtime at $1.40. Hiring halls would be maintained jointly by the employers and the union but, significantly, selection of the dispatcher was left solely to the union.

The unemployed and other workers who had participated were tremendously encouraged by the victory. Julia Ruutilla, a longtime Portland labor activist, pointed out that the strike "was sort of the mainspring for everyone that wanted to organize industrial-type of unions." For example, saw mills all over Portland organized in the wake of the strike. Textile workers and loggers also renewed their organizing efforts.

The longshoremen's achievement helped shatter the myth that employers, backed by the force of the police, would always win. Other unions realized the vast power of an active rank and file in alliance with the larger working-class community—though subsequent events proved that the lesson has not always stuck.

The shenanigans of ILA President Joseph Ryan were sharp reminders that, but for the union's democratic structure, the strike would have been lost—"sold out" would be the term given by longshoremen. Following the strike, Portland's Local 8 adopted a number of rules in an effort to assure the vitality of this democracy: No one could be a union official who was not a full-time working longshoreman. The tenure of office was held to one year, and salaried officials were prohibited from succeeding themselves or rotating to other paid positions. All major decisions of the executive board had to be approved at a membership meeting before being acted upon. To assure the meeting would represent the feelings of the workers, attendance was made mandatory.

Born out of a struggle in which participants learned to care, look out for, and trust one another, the union's official slogan became: "An injury to one is an injury to all."

STUDENT HANDOUT #14

UNION MAIDS
Letter from a Relative

Dear Kate,

I'm sorry to hear you are so sick. I know it must be hard to be in poor health, alone and having to look back on your life.

Kate, I wish that you had really made something of your life. With your brains you could have been a lawyer or a doctor. You really could have accomplished important things in your life. But Kate, I don't even think you had fun.

I know that you must regret as much as I do that you got mixed up in that silly union stuff. It must be very painful for you to think about what a waste it all was.

I don't mean to make you more depressed. But this was on my mind and I love you so much I just had to tell you.

Your cousin,

Helen

Assignment

Kate is the older woman in the film *Union Maids*. Put yourself in her position. You're now seventy years old. You've just received the letter above from a close relative. Write a detailed reply to Helen challenging her assertion that your life was a waste. Try to explain why you believe your life has had meaning. Use examples—you can either use stories she told in the film or make up events that could have taken place.

STUDENT HANDOUT #15-A

PLANT CLOSURES FACT SHEET

What are Plant Closures? Plant closures are the complete or partial shutdown of business operations, permanently or indefinitely. They may occur in offices, factories, mills, retail stores, hotels, supermarkets, or other businesses.

For the Laid-Off Workers, Closures Often Mean:

—Little notice or warning and no severance pay.

—Loss of pensions and health benefits.

—Increased medical problems and life-threatening diseases:

(1) an increase in ulcers, a greater likelihood of future heart ailments, greater hypertension and other illnesses sensitive to stress, such as diabetes and asthma;

(2) a suicide rate thirty times the national average;

(3) mental health problems stemming from a loss of self-esteem and feelings of uselessness; increased admissions to mental health institutions;

(4) increased alcohol and drug abuse.

For the Families and Communities:

—Increased instances of child abuse, malnutrition, battered wives, and divorce.

—Higher rates of serious crime, both as victims and perpetrators.

—Greater demand for public benefit programs and services and fewer tax revenues to pay for the programs.

—Lost purchasing power in the community, leading to additional lost jobs in retail business, wholesale, transport, services, as well as among the suppliers of the plant being closed.

—Family and community life broken up as husbands, wives, or families leave to search for work elsewhere.

—A possibly hazardous site left behind.

When new jobs can be found, they often are in lower skilled, lower paying industries.

Why Plant Closures Happen:

There is no single reason. Closures used to happen primarily in economic hard times. Now the business being closed is often still profitable. The corporation may be moving to an area of the United States or of the world where it can pay lower wages or avoid unions. U.S. tax laws provide incentives for businesses to relocate, even overseas. Sometimes corporations use the *threat* of closure as a way of bargaining with employees to lower wages or reduce protections in a union contract.

STUDENT HANDOUT #15-B

FIRST RESPONSES

It was just one week ago that you first heard about the closure and you're still in a state of shock. Supervisors gathered groups of workers together during first shift in the steel mill where you work and announced that the mill would soon be closing. You've worked there for fifteen and a half years. Your father works there. So do some of your cousins and many of your neighbors. Some families have three generations working there at the same time.

Rob Engelhart

"It's not as if it's a complete surprise," says the owner of the grocery where your family shops. For years she's let you buy on credit. Now she and other storeowners are asking customers to pay in cash. "We've heard about other mills being shut, and the company threatened to close last time you were in negotiations."

That's part of what upsets you. Your union has a history of fighting for improvements in working conditions. Last negotiations, the union agreed to give up work rules that it had gained years ago. You're now doing your own maintenance on equipment that breaks down instead of waiting for a maintenance person to come and fix it. And the members accepted a contract with no increase in pay. In exchange, the company agreed to try to keep the mill open.

When you graduated from high school you didn't think twice about a different career. Steelmaking was hard work and it was dirty. It made the community around the mill dirty too. But the mills had been running for decades. It seemed like they'd go forever. By this time, steelmaking is most of what you know. "What other kind of job can I do?" you think to yourself. "Is there other work available? Where will I have to move?"

Your kids are still a little young to have to decide about jobs, although they're old enough to earn some spending money in the summers. They've bounced baseballs off your steel-toed boots and breathed the red dust and walked with you around the mill. When they were smaller, one of them bragged to her friends that you personally had "made the steel that's in our car." You've not encouraged them one way or the other, but until now it wouldn't have surprised you if one or both of them had ended up working alongside you in the mill.

That day after work, some of the men were so

angry that they smashed their hardhats against the wall. Most didn't feel like talking. They seemed to be asking themselves how they were going to break the news to their families. If their response was anything like yours, they also were blaming themselves: "How are we going to keep up the house payments? What am I good for if I can't bring home a paycheck any longer?"

The supervisor read a letter from the president of the company. It said that the mill was closing because other mills were making steel more cheaply in countries like Korea and Brazil. Although the mill was still profitable, it couldn't make enough money while there was "unfair competition" from abroad. The letter also said that the mill was old and that laws about pollution were becoming stricter. It would cost too much to install new scrubbers in the smokestacks to reduce pollution.

Within a couple of days, somebody had written a petition: "We, the undersigned, ask the President and Congress to restrict imports of steel, to relax environmental standards, and to permit the American steel industry to EARN A FAIR PROFIT." Thousands of people, both workers and community residents, signed the petition, and it was sent off with a caravan of cars to Washington, D.C. The President, however, did not meet with the petitioners. After marching around the White House for a few hours, they returned home, the petition undelivered.

Some of your friends have had second thoughts about the petition. "Why make demands on the government?" they say. "It's not the government that decided to close our mill. Anyway, those demands are just what the company wants." These friends are talking about more direct action against the company. Can the company be persuaded or forced to keep the mill open?

Others, especially some of the older workers, are reluctant to rock the boat. After decades of work, they don't want to take actions that might threaten their pensions. You've noticed that the union's health and safety committee has suddenly become less active. They seem to think that if the company gets less pressure from workers, management might reconsider and stay open. You've got to keep working there for now, however, and you're becoming uneasy about worsening conditions.

Even some of the younger workers don't feel any urgency. "There's plenty of financial aid available," they say. The union has already scheduled workshops on how to apply for unemployment compensation and for the layoff benefits in the contract with the company. You know those benefits will quickly run out. You're also worried about divisions that are developing between older and younger workers, those with different financial stakes and different understandings of who's to blame.

Somebody you know has printed bumper stickers that say "IF YOU LOSE YOUR JOB, BLAME IT ON AN ENVIRONMENTALIST." You took some to distribute, but are now uncertain. You've always loved the outdoors, and you know the air and water, the woods and the wildlife, have been hurt by pollution from the mill.

Within the past week, various community groups have become involved. "This isn't only a problem for the millworkers and their families," one of the local ministers says. "The whole community will be devastated." Women's groups, religious organizations, organizations of minorities, all are talking about the situation. Public employees have already been told that some of them will be laid off if the mill closes, because there won't be enough tax revenues to continue some public programs. And the teachers' union has sent a message of support to your union, saying they know the quality of education is at stake as well as their own members' jobs.

Assignment

Everybody seems to have a different idea for what should be done. Write an interior monologue of your own first responses, your feelings as well as your ideas. How have your thoughts changed in the week since you heard the bad news? Why?

STUDENT HANDOUT #15-C

PLANT CLOSURE LEGISLATION
Option Sheet

A number of European countries have laws that limit a company's right to close a business operation. U.S. companies are present in all these countries and operate under their laws. Usually these laws apply only to companies that employ a certain number of workers, more than two hundred, for instance. All of them require that the company give advance notice of any shutdown, sixty days, for example, or one year, so that workers will have time to look for another job or that unions and governments will have time to try to keep the operation open. Some of the laws require severance benefits, payments by the company to workers who are being laid off. Some require the company to pay money into a community assistance fund. Other features that appear in some of the laws include: paid leaves for workers to look for new employment; government assistance to employee efforts to buy the plant and keep it running; the right of workers to relocate to other operations of the same company. The following questions investigate the idea of plant closure legislation.

Note: You are under no obligation to support this option, only to investigate it fairly. You may even end up opposing it.

—If we were to support a plant closure law, what feature should it contain. Some of those above? All of those above? Others in addition?

In some states where there have been campaigns for plant closure laws, people have sent thousands of pre-printed postcards to the legislature. In some, full-time union officials have lobbied legislators, taking them to lunch, promising to support them on other issues in ex-change for their support on this. In Montana, there was an initiative campaign. Thousands of workers discussed the issues in union meetings, then went door-to-door talking with their neighbors, collecting signatures. If they had been successful, the initiative would have appeared on a statewide ballot for everyone to vote on instead of going to the legislature.

—There are different strategies behind each of these plans. Some methods try to educate people; some trust the unions to get their members active. Others rely more on government and union officials. What would be the best way or ways to work for a law?

—A group of local businesspeople is very opposed to plant closure legislation. They say that if we pass that law in our state, new businesses won't locate here. How would we respond to this argument?

—We are confronted by a group of workers who say that large severance benefits may discourage workers from looking for any alternative to a shutdown. Are they right? Explain.

—*The Wall Street Journal*, a national newspaper primarily for businesspeople, has editorialized that plant closure laws take away the rights of companies and may even force them to lose money. They want to know why some people should be allowed to take away the rights of others.

—What questions do we still have about whether or not plant closure legislation is a good idea?

STUDENT HANDOUT #15-D

GOVERNMENT RELIEF FOR THE COMPANIES
Option Sheet

Even though ours is called a "free enterprise" economy, government assistance to companies is quite common. In the United States, government is a major buyer of products. Much of the research in developing new materials and products is done with government support. Local, state, and national governments play roles in training people to be workers. This assistance happens, of course, through the use of taxes that individuals and companies pay.

There also are many instances of government aid to companies having economic difficulties: tax reductions or allowing the company not to pay local property taxes; loans at low interest rates; freeing the company from having to comply with environmental standards; restricting imports that compete with the company's products. Here we investigate the option of government assistance.

Note: You are under no obligation to support this option, only to investigate it fairly. You may even end up opposing it.

—We've already been part of a petition campaign that asked the national government "to restrict imports of steel" and "to relax environmental standards." Do we still think that these are good requests? Are there additional kinds of government relief we could request?

—After the petition campaign, a lot of union members began to believe that it was a mistake to join forces with the company. They say that accepting the company's program prevents us from fighting to change the shutdown decision. What do we think about this argument?

—A lot of our members and community people are feeling that they can't affect what happens, that the company holds power. Asking the government for aid simply puts everything in the government's hands. Is it possible for us to develop a campaign for aid that doesn't just leave all the power with the government? If so, how?

—In a number of instances, companies have simply taken advantage of government relief. Playskool, a Chicago manufacturer of educational toys, received a lower tax rate and a loan from the city. It promised to stay open and to hire new workers. Instead, it used the money to bring in equipment replacing workers. Then it transferred its operations to another state where it could pay lower wages. Any government agency that we approach will want to know how this kind of abuse can be prevented. If we favor government relief, what can we suggest?

—What questions do we still have about obtaining government relief for the company?

STUDENT HANDOUT #15-E

TAKE OVER THE PLANT AND RUN IT OURSELVES
Option Sheet

When a large aerospace company in Britain decided to close one of its plants, workers came up with a way to keep it open. "If the old products aren't selling well," they said, "we'll use our knowledge and skills to develop new products and keep our jobs." Based on the same technologies that had been creating products for the military, the unions at Lucas Aerospace set up committees among their members to design products and processes that would be both socially useful and ecologically sound. They were so successful in their ideas that unions in other large companies adopted the same approach to threatened closures. Ultimately, the management of the companies kept control and the workers' ideas were not carried out. Their struggle, however, showing the possibility of staying open, did prevent some of the announced shutdowns.

In one Ralston Purina plant that made animal food in the United States, there was so much resistance to management by the workers that the company agreed to an experiment. They removed all management, all supervisors, all foremen, and let the workers organize production and run the plant themselves. Productivity steadily increased; so did the company's profits. The experiment was such a success that the company ended it, fearing to lose control of this plant and other plants. Here are some questions about this option.

Note: You are under no obligation to support this option, only to investigate it fairly. You may even end up opposing it.

—Consultants in situations similar to ours have suggested that there are many ways a takeover could occur. Our own pension funds could be used for an "employee stock ownership plan." Local government could use the "right of eminent domain," paying a fair market price and forcing the company to sell the plant. The federal government could lend money, keeping some sort of public ownership. Pension funds from other unions could invest in the mill. Which of these plans seems to offer the most hope? Why? What further questions do we have?

—If we somehow were in a position to run our mill without the company, how would we organize production? Would we still have supervisors? What kind of management might we need or want? How would these decisions be made?

—Would we still have the union or would it no longer be necessary?

—The company has been unable to make a profit it considers acceptable. Would our needs for profit be the same as those of the company? (Remember that there would still have to be money coming in not only for paychecks but to repair or replace expensive equipment.)

—Some of our members who support a takeover see the goal as having a steelmill that can compete effectively with other steelmills. Other supporters see the goal as showing workers everywhere a better way of working together. For them, the process of fighting for the takeover and developing the vision of a mill run by the workers is a way of overcoming the powerlessness that many feel. It may not be possible to accomplish both goals. What differences do we see between them, and how would we respond to each group?

—What questions do we still have about taking over the plant and running it ourselves?

STUDENT HANDOUT #15-F

PERSUADE OR FORCE THE COMPANY TO STAY
Option Sheet

Unions have adopted very different tactics in trying to prevent a threatened shutdown. In some instances they have granted concessions, agreed to accept lower wages or benefits or to change the work rules in favor of management. Sometimes concessions have been given in exchange for shares in the company or a share of future profits. There also have been times when companies used the money they had gained from concessions to expand their operations elsewhere or even move equipment to other locations before shutting the original plant.

Note: You are under no obligation to support this option, only to investigate it fairly. You may even end up opposing it.

—In our last negotiations, we had to grant concessions on work rules and wages. Clearly these weren't enough. If the company were willing to consider keeping the mill open in exchange for further concessions, what might we offer?

—What would we expect or demand in return?

—Even at the last negotiations, a lot of our members opposed concessions. They argued that if we lowered our wages or weakened our work rules, workers in other mills would have to do the same in order for their mills to stay competitive. We would just be competing with other workers in an endless cycle of lowering our living conditions. At the first mention of concessions, these members are likely to raise the same argument. Are they right or wrong? Why?

—In other instances unions have refused to give concessions and have tried, sometimes successfully, to force the company to stay open. In Minneapolis, a coalition of church, farmer, and labor groups joined to boycott Northrup King's seed company and other products, such as Ovaltine and Ex-Lax, made by its owner. In Chicago, the union got a court order stopping U.S. Steel from tearing down a plant until there was a chance to explore alternatives. Morse Cutting Tool in Massachusetts asked for concessions, then used them to begin moving machinery to another plant. The union refused additional concessions, went on strike, and mounted a campaign showing how the health of the entire community would be threatened by a shutdown. Seniors' organizations, clergymen, university faculty, and other unions all joined together. When the company tried to bring pressure, for example to cut off insurance to the strikers, solid community support forced the company to back down. Eventually, with the threat of a takeover by the city using the right of eminent domain, the company sold the plant to another company that has kept it open. What kind of pressure can we put on the company to keep it open?

—Many of our members feel that there is little we can do, that the big decisions are up to the company or the government. Are there actions we could take that could be effective and might also inspire rather than demoralize members?

—What questions do we still have about trying to persuade or force the company to stay?

STUDENT HANDOUT #15-G

THE ACTION IS TODAY

Along with your family and neighbors, you're attending a community rally in Youngstown, Ohio. Two major steel mills in town have already been closed. Your friends and relatives who worked in them tried everything: lawsuits and lobbying, demonstrations and delegations. Now U.S. Steel has announced it is shutting another mill.

The first speakers are politicians, there to get your support for new legislation or to take credit for their opposition to shutdowns. Someone gives a talk on welfare benefits. The crowd is restless. Then the president of a local, most of whose members have left the union because their mill was shut, begins to speak:

"I'm not interested in calling a lot of people together and just talking to them and going home. I think we've got a job to do today. And that job is to let U.S. Steel know that this is the end of the line. No more jobs are going to be shut down in Youngstown.

"You've got men here, you've got women here, you've got children here, and we're here for one purpose. Not to be talked to about what's going to happen in Congress two years from now. What's going to happen in Youngstown today? There's a building two blocks from here. That's the U.S. Steel headquarters. You know the whole country is looking at the voters, the citizens. What are you going to do? Are you going to take action, or are you going to sit and talk and be talked to?

"The action is today. We're going down that hill, and we're going to let the politicians know, we're going to let U.S. Steel know, we're going to let the whole country know that steelworkers in Youngstown got guts and we want to fight for our jobs. We're not going to fight for welfare!

"In 1919 the fight was on for the eight-hour day and they lost that struggle and they burned down East Youngstown, which is the Campbell steel mill. Now I'm not saying burn anything down, but you got the eight-hour day.

"In 1937 you wanted a union and people got shot in Youngstown because they wanted a union. And everything hasn't been that great since you got that union. Every day you put your life on the line when you went into that iron house. Every day you sucked up the dirt and took a chance on breaking your legs or breaking your back. And anyone who's worked in there knows what I'm talking about.

"Now I don't like to read to people but in 1857 Frederick Douglass said something that I think you ought to listen to: *Those who profess to favor freedom and yet discourage agitation are men who want crops without plowing up the ground. They want rain without thunder and lightning. They want the ocean without the awful roar of its waters. This struggle may be a moral one* [and you've heard a lot about that] *or it may be a physical one* [and you're going to hear about that] *but it must be a struggle. Power concedes nothing without a demand. It never did and it never will. Find out what people will submit to and you will find out the exact measure of injustice and wrong which will be imposed upon them. And these will be continued until they are resisted with either words or blows or with both. The limits of tyrants are prescribed by the endurance of those they oppress.*

"This was said in 1857 and things haven't changed. U.S. Steel is going to see how much they can put on you. And when I say 'you' I mean Youngstown, you know. We've got lists. We've got an obituary of plants that were shut down in the last twenty years. When are we going to make a stand?

"Now, I'm going down that hill and I'm going into that building. And anyone that doesn't want to come along doesn't have to, but I'm sure there are those who'll want to. And one thing we're going to do when we get in there, we're going to stay there until they meet with the president of the local."

When he finishes, the president of the union that called the rally speaks briefly: "Like Ed told you, there's no free lunch. You've got to fight for what you want. We've been trying to talk to U.S. Steel. They won't listen to us. We've been trying to talk to the president. He won't talk to us. We have to make these people listen!

"If U.S. Steel doesn't want to make steel in Youngstown, the people of Youngstown will make steel in Youngstown! We're going down that hill!"*

---

*From Staughton Lynd, *The Fight Against Shutdowns: Youngstown's Steel Mill Closings* (San Pedro, CA: Singlejack Books, 1982).

Assignment

Complete one of the following:

1. Imagine that you are the main speaker quoted above. You attended the "union meetings" held in class. Write a letter to class members explaining your reaction to the decisions they reached. Include in the letter your reaction to the way they arrived at their decisions.

    or

2. Staying in your role as a union member, write a letter to the main speaker explaining in detail your response to the action proposed above. What are the advantages or disadvantages that you see in that action?

STUDENT HANDOUT #16

LABOR SONGS

Solidarity Forever

(Written by Ralph Chaplin, January 1915. Sung to the tune of "John Brown's Body")

When the Union's inspiration through the workers' blood shall run,
There can be no power greater anywhere beneath the sun.
Yet what force on earth is weaker than the feeble strength of one?
But the Union makes us strong.

Solidarity forever!
Solidarity forever!
Solidarity forever!
For the Union makes us strong.

Is there aught we hold in common with the greedy parasite
Who would lash us into serfdom and would crush us with his might?
Is there anything left to us but to organize and fight?
For the Union makes us strong.
[Chorus]

It is we who plowed the prairies; built the cities where they trade;
Dug the mines and built the workshops; endless miles of railroad laid.
Now we stand outcast and starving, 'midst the wonder we have made;
But the Union makes us strong.
[Chorus]

All the world that's owned by idle drones is ours and ours alone.
We have laid the wide foundations; built it skyward stone by stone.
It is ours, not to slave in, but to master and to own,
While the Union makes us strong.
[Chorus]

They have taken untold millions that they never toiled to earn,
But without our brain and muscle not a single wheel can turn.
We can break their haughty power; gain our freedom when we learn
That the Union makes us strong.
[Chorus]

In our hands is placed a power greater than their hoarded gold;
Greater than the might of armies, magnified a thousand-fold.
We can bring to birth a new world from the ashes of the old.
For the Union makes us strong.
[Chorus]

Union Maid

(Sung to the tune of "Red Wing." *Words:* Verses 1 & 2: Woody Guthrie; Verse 3: Nancy Katz; Verses 4–8: Jan Mandell, Lori Hanson, Sue Kroll for the Twin Cities Women's Union)

There once was a union maid who never was afraid
Of the goons and ginks and company finks
And the deputy sheriff who made the raid.
She went to the union hall when a meeting it was called
And when the company boys came round
She always stood her ground:

Chorus:
Oh, you can't scare me, I'm sticking to the union,
I'm sticking to the union, I'm sticking to the union.
Oh, you can't scare me, I'm sticking to the union
I'm sticking to the union til the day I die.
(Repeat chorus after each verse)

This union maid was wise to the tricks of company spies
She wouldn't be fooled by company stools,
She'd always organize the guys.
She'd always get her way when she struck for higher pay.
She'd show her card to the National Guard,
And this is what she'd say:

A woman's struggle is hard even with a union card
She's got to stand on her own two feet
And not be a servant of the male elite.
It's time to take a stand, keep working hand in hand,
There's a job that's got to be done
And a fight that's got to be won.
We all were once alone, the U.S. we did roam
Isolated from each other, sister, wife and grandmother.
But now the time has come, for us to become one.
That's why we all are here today, and now it's time to say:

So women did unite and we began to fight.
From office, home and factory, demanding our equality.
Oh yes there was a day we struck for higher pay
Now we say that we want more
So listen to us roar:

We'll build a union strong to help us move along.
We won't stand still together we
Will turn this system all around.
Now women take the lead to meet the people's need
Join hand in hand and take a stand
And we'll control the land.

Casey Jones—The Union Scab

(By Joe Hill; sung to the tune of "Casey Jones")

The workers on the S.P. line to strike sent out a call;
But Casey Jones, the engineer, he wouldn't strike at all;
His boiler it was leaking, and its drivers on the bum,
And his engine and its bearings, they were all out of plumb.

Casey Jones kept his junk pile running;
Casey Jones was working double time;
Casey Jones got a wooden medal,
For being good and faithful on the S.P. line.

The workers said to Casey; "Won't you help us win this strike?"
But Casey said: "Let me alone, you'd better take a hike."
Then Casey's wheezy engine ran right off the worn-out track,
And Casey hit the river with an awful crack.

Casey Jones hit the river bottom;
Casey Jones broke his blooming spine;
Casey Jones was an Angeleno,
He took a trip to heaven on the S.P. line.

When Casey Jones got up to heaven to the Pearly Gate,
He said: "I'm Casey Jones, the guy that pulled the S.P. freight."
"You're just the man," said Peter, "our musicians went on strike;
You can get a job a-scabbing any time you like."

Casey Jones got a job in heaven;
Casey Jones was doing mighty fine;
Casey Jones went scabbing on the angels,
Just like he did to workers on the S.P. line.

The angels got together and they said it wasn't fair
For Casey Jones to go around a-scabbing everywhere.
The Angel Union No. 23, they sure were there,
And they promptly fired Casey down the Golden Stair.

Casey Jones went to Hell a-flying;
"Casey Jones," the Devil said, "Oh fine;
Casey Jones, get busy shoveling sulphur—
That's what you get for scabbing on the S.P. line."

Hallelujah, I'm a Bum!

(This is a hobo parody of the last century, adapted by Spokane IWW in the winter of 1908 for use on song cards. Sung to the tune of "Revive Us Again.")

O, why don't you work
Like other men do?
How in hell can I work
When there's no work to do?

Chorus:
Hallelujah, I'm a bum!
Hallelujah, bum again!
Hallelujah, give us a handout
To revive us again.

O, why don't you save
All the money you earn?
If I did not eat
I'd have money to burn.
(Chorus)

O, I like my boss—
He's a good friend of mine;
That's why I am starving
Out in the breadline.
(Chorus)

I can't buy a job
For I ain't got the dough,
So I ride in a box-car
For I'm a hobo.
(Chorus)

Whenever I get
All the money I earn
The boss will be broke
And to work he must turn.
(Chorus)

SELECTED FURTHER READING

The following titles are not meant as a complete bibliography but are listed as useful background readings for the different units in the curriculum.

Unit I: Basic Understandings

Richard O. Boyer and Herbert M. Morais, *Labor's Untold Story* (New York: United Electrical, Radio, and Machine Workers of America, 1955).

Jeremy Brecher, *Strike!* (Boston: South End Press, 1977).

Paul Buhle and Alan Dawley, eds., *Working for Democracy: American Workers from the Revolution to the Present* (Urbana: University of Illinois Press, 1985).

James R. Green, *The World of the Worker: Labor in Twentieth Century America* (New York: Hill and Wang, 1980).

Staughton Lynd, *Labor Law for the Rank and Filer* (San Pedro, CA: Singlejack Books, 1978).

Unit II: Changes in the Workplace/"Scientific Management"

Harry Braverman, *Labor and Monopoly Capital: The Degradation of Work in the Twentieth Century* (New York: Monthly Review Press, 1974).

Eric Breitbart (producer), *Clockwork* (25 minutes), 1981; distributed by California Newsreel (630 Natoma St., San Francisco, CA 94103).

Stuart Ewen, *Captains of Consciousness: Advertising and the Social Roots of Consumer Culture* (New York: McGraw-Hill, 1976).

Milton Meltzer, *Bread and Roses: The Struggle of American Labor, 1865–1915* (New York: Vintage, 1973).

Unit III: Defeats, Victories, Challenges

Rosalyn Baxandall, Linda Gordon, Susan Reverby, eds., *America's Working Women: A Documentary History— 1600 to the Present* (New York: Vintage, 1976).

David Brody, *Steelworkers in America: The Nonunion Era* (New York: Harper and Row, 1960).

William Cahn, *Lawrence 1912: The Bread and Roses Strike* (New York: The Pilgrim Press, 1977).

Joyce L. Kornbluh, ed., *Rebel Voices: An IWW Anthology* (Chicago: Charles H. Kerr, 1988).

Meredith Tax, *The Rising of the Women: Feminist Solidarity and Class Conflict, 1880–1917* (New York: Monthly Review Press, 1980).

Unit IV: Our Own Recent Past

Alice and Staughton Lynd, eds., *Rank and File: Personal Histories by Working-Class Organizers* (New York: Monthly Review Press, 1988).

Marc S. Miller, ed., *Working Lives: The* Southern Exposure *History of Labor in the South* (New York: Pantheon Books, 1980).

H.L. Mitchell, *Roll the Union On: A Pictorial History of the Southern Tenant Farmers' Union* (Chicago: Charles H. Kerr, 1987).

Mike Quin, *The Big Strike* (New York: International Publishers, 1949). (On the 1934 Longshore strike.)

Unit V: Continuing Struggle

Larry Adelman (producer), *Controlling Interest: The World of the Multinational Corporation* (43 minutes), 1978; distributed by California Newsreel (630 Natoma Street, San Francisco, CA 94103).

Marc Freeman, Claire Shoen, Jack Wilson (producers), *Mad River: Hard Times in Humboldt County* (56 minutes), 1982; distributed by California Newsreel (630 Natoma Street, San Francisco, CA 94103).

Industrial Workers of the World, *Songs of the Workers* (Chicago, nd.).

Staughton Lynd, *The Fight Against Shutdowns; Youngstown's Steel Mill Closings* (San Pedro, CA: Singlejack Books, 1982).

A good source of information about ongoing labor activities is *Labor Notes,* a monthly journal of news and analysis available from Labor Education and Research Project, 7435 Michigan Avenue, Detroit, Michigan 48210.

Many of the readings listed in the above categories also pertain to continuing labor struggles.

———————————

Suggested readings and resources on teaching critical thinking and democratic values:

William Bigelow, *Strangers in Their Own Country: A Curriculum Guide on South Africa* (Trenton, NJ: Africa World Press, 1985).

Violence, the Ku Klux Klan, and the Struggle for Equality, Connecticut Education Association, Council on Interracial Books for Children, and the National Education Association, 1981.

Ellen Davidson and Nancy Schniedewind, *Cooperative Learning, Cooperative Lives: A Sourcebook of Learning Activities for Building a Peaceful World* (Dubuque, Iowa: Wm. C. Brown, 1987).

Paolo Freire, *Pedagogy of the Oppressed* (New York: Continuum, 1970).

Paolo Freire and Ira Shor, *A Pedagogy for Liberation: Dialogues on Transforming Education* (Amherst, MA: Bergin and Garvey, 1987).

Barbara Gates, Susan Klaw, and Adria Steinberg, *Changing Learning, Changing Lives: A High School Women's Studies Curriculum from the Group School* (New York: The Feminist Press, 1979).

Ira Shor, *Critical Teaching and Everyday Life* (Chicago: University of Chicago Press, 1980).

Sonja Williams, *Exploding the Hunger Myths: A High School Curriculum* (San Francisco: Food First, 1987).

EVALUATION

Please take some time to complete the following evaluation. We will put all respondents on a mailing list to receive additional information about the curriculum or lessons of interest.

1. Describe the class or group with whom you used *The Power in Our Hands:* ages of students, backgrounds, other areas of study, numbers of students involved, etc.

2. Which lessons from the curriculum did you use?

3. Apart from specific information, what were the major ideas and concepts you think your students learned from participating in the lessons?

4. Are there lessons you developed to supplement the lessons in *The Power in Our Hands?* Please describe these in some detail and enclose any readings or handouts you developed.

5. For a future edition of *The Power in Our Hands,* what improvements and additions would you suggest?

Name _____

Address _____

_____

School or institution: _____

Return to: Curriculum Workshop, 734 S.E. Lexington, Portland, OR 97202.

NOTES

Norman Diamond is former executive director of the Pacific Northwest Labor College. He has worked in a steel mill, saw mill, and as a college professor. His writing on cultural criticism, social movements, and science and technology focuses on how values and understandings change.

William Bigelow is the author of the acclaimed curriculum guide to South Africa, *Strangers in Their Own Country,* as well as articles on educational issues. He is a teacher at Jefferson High School in Portland, Oregon.

The authors began their collaboration on this book nearly a decade ago. They have developed and successfully used these lessons in high school and university courses, labor studies and union education programs, and together with leaders of community, black, and women's groups.